9 ✓

HISTORY &FAITH

A Personal Exploration

Colin Brown

D0104568

Academie
Books Grand Rapids.
        Michigan
Zondervan Publishing House

HISTORY AND FAITH
Copyright © 1987 by Colin Brown

ACADEMIE BOOKS
is an imprint of
Zondervan Publishing House
1415 Lake Drive, S.E.
Grand Rapids, Michigan 49506

Library of Congress Cataloging in Publication Data

Brown, Colin, 1932–
   History and faith.

   Bibliography: p.
   1. History (Theology)   I. Title.

BR115.H5B68 1987   231.7′6   87–14579
ISBN   0–310–21961–2

Edited by Ed van der Maas
Designed by Louise Bauer

Printed in the United States of America

88 89 90 91 92 / CH / 10 9 8 7 6 5 4 3 2

Contents

Preface

History and Faith is a revision of a study that first appeared over a decade ago. In its earlier form it was entitled "History and the Believer," and it formed part of a book I edited which was called *History, Criticism and Faith: Four Exploratory Studies.*[1] In revising my study for separate publication I have not attempted to incorporate what my colleagues said in their studies. Nor have I attempted to develop a philosophy of history. I have kept with my original theme, and I refer those who are interested in particular questions to follow them up in the works mentioned in my endnotes and bibliography. Likewise, I have resisted the temptation to enlarge my study by responding to the many important books and articles on the subject of history that have appeared in the last ten years.[2] These works deserve to be read in their own right.

To have turned my study into what scholars call a *Forschungsbericht*, a state-of-the-art report on research, would have changed its character. It would doubtless have gained in providing information and comment on sundry issues, but it would have been at the price of making my work unwieldy. There is a real need for a thorough review of thinking about history and an appraisal of current techniques and methods, but the present study is not the right vehicle. To attempt to turn it into such would be like trying to make a Volkswagen Beetle into a Rolls Royce.

There are two main reasons why I have not radically altered the shape of my study. The first is that I did not want to complicate the argument more than necessary. The second is my conviction that the basic argument was sound. I have, however, changed the title. The original title sounded a bit defensive and inward looking. What I have to say will, I hope, be of some interest to others besides believers who may feel threatened by historical scholarship. I have attempted to set forth for Christian believers and for anyone else who might be interested the issues as I see them. I have done some rewriting in order to bring out the importance of points and have made numerous changes of detail. Where appropriate I have responded in the endnotes to the scholarship of the last ten years. In various places I have worked into the text references to recent writing and to up-to-date critical editions of works used in the first version of my study. A case in point is the use of the new Princeton edition of Kierkegaard's *Philosophical Fragments.* Perhaps the most significant addition to this revision of my study is the "Note on the Gospel Miracles" at the end of the book. I have included this material as a separate note to avoid disrupting the flow of the argument in chapter 1. It calls attention to an argument, developed more fully in my books *Miracles and the Critical Mind*[3] and *That You May Believe,*[4] that cuts across a number of accepted attitudes to the gospel miracle stories.

Introduction: Why Should We Bother About History?

A faith that does not touch life is not worth having. Biblical religion has never been simply a matter of giving mental assent to esoteric ideas. From its beginning Christianity has stressed the outworking of faith in life. The Christian message deliberately aims to change lives and attitudes. Christians today should be concerned with the whole range of social questions no less than with the spread of the gospel and the full riches of God's gifts and power, but the big danger in all this is that of turning Christianity into a form of existentialism. I do not mean the philosophical kind of existentialism with its technical jargon, its lengthy abstract analysis of the structure of being, and its talk about the difference between authentic and inauthentic existence. Rather, it is an unphilosophical, practical kind of existentialism in which questions of daily existence not only take precedence over but crowd out the deeper questions of being and truth. "Will it work?" is more often asked than "Is it true?" "Do I feel good about it?" is felt to be more important than "What grounds are there for thinking this?" "Will people buy it?" replaces "Have we tested it?"

In this process even some of the most conservative Christians can come out looking like Bultmannians. Rudolf Bultmann, the German scholar who dominated theology in the postwar era, was highly skeptical about the historical value of the New Testament. He believed that we could know very little about what Jesus was really like. Jesus and his message were merely the *presupposition* for the theology of the New Testament rather than part of that theology itself.[1] Conservative Christians might be surprised to be told that they come across like Bultmannians, especially if they know something about Bultmann. But in practice we all need to face up to the question of whether Jesus is anything more than a presupposition in our thinking or, worse still, a pretext for our actions. If Jesus is no more than a *presupposition*, what are we to make of the whole superstructure of beliefs, attitudes, and practices that is built on it?

Through the ages Christianity has presented itself as a historical religion. It is based on claims about what God has done in history. It centers on claims such as that of John 3:16 that "God so loved the world that he gave his one and only Son, that whoever believes in him shall not perish but have eternal life." Christian attitudes toward social and moral questions, toward the spread of the Christian message, and toward spirituality are all rooted and grounded in history. History is the foundation and center of the Christian faith, but many modern Christians appear to be unconcerned with history in their pursuit of more tangible objectives; and skeptics and opponents have long tried to undermine the historical foundations of the Christian faith. If Christianity can in practice be cut loose from its supposed historical foundations, what is its value? Perhaps, after all, it is a body of comforting myths that enables us to come to terms with the harsh realities of life and a set of beliefs that can be brought out from time to time to reinforce attitudes.

The eighteenth-century German dramatist, literary critic, and amateur theologian Gotthold Ephraim Lessing once remarked that "accidental truths of history can never become the proof of necessary truths of reason."[2] The dictum was propounded in the heat of argument, but it has been remembered long after the particular argument has been forgotten, because it focuses on a problem. History—both in the sense of what *happened* in the past and in the sense of *accounts of* the past—seems to be so much less solid than, say, Pythagoras's theorem or the proposition that two and two make four. It is not self-evident like the latter. Nor can it be proved like scientific theories. The scientist verifies his hypotheses in a laboratory by controlled experiments. His findings and his methods can be checked by anyone who can understand what is involved and who can perform similar experiments. Compared with that, history seems so insecure with its dependence on witnesses, second-hand and third-hand evidence, documents whose survival seems to depend so much on chance, and the rival interpretations of historians. To bring God into it only seems to make the whole undertaking doubly dubious. For Lessing history could never provide the foundation for religious faith. At best it could tell us what religious people said and did and so provide historical illustrations of truths that had to be discovered by reason reflecting on experience.

Whether we agree with Lessing or not, we cannot get away from history. What William the Conqueror, Christopher Columbus, and Adolf Hitler did in their different ways has affected the lives of all of us in the modern world. The more we understand the past, the better we are able to find our way about the present. But how are we to understand the past? Are we to see history through the eyes of a Marxist? And if so, which brand of Marxist? Christians talk about seeing things in a Christian perspective, but are not these terms loaded, and are not the various slants that people bring to history all more or less arbitrary and not part of history itself? Christians talk about God in history, but can any self-respecting historian today bring himself to use such language without throwing overboard the very rules of the game?

This book is concerned with these kinds of questions. My aim is not to try to summarize the results of historical scholarship but rather to set forth my personal exploration of how historical study affects faith. The four chapters of this book look at four areas of debate. Chapter 1 begins with a preliminary survey of the question of "God in History," for this is the crunch question for the Christian and anyone looking at the Christian faith. I ask what it means to talk about God in history and offer some thoughts on the problems presented by stories about miracles such as we find in the gospel accounts of Jesus. This leads to the question of criteria and methods which I examine in chapter 2 under the heading of "Rules, Principles, and Explanations." Here too the main interest lies in asking what bearing these have on taking seriously the idea of God and the supernatural in history. Chapter 3, "What Does the Historian Achieve?" has to do with what is often but loosely called historical reconstruction. Chapter 4, "How Does History Affect Belief?" focuses on (1) history and revelation and (2) the importance of history to the believer. In 'A Note on the Gospel Miracles' I examine some often-overlooked features of the New Testament accounts of Jesus' miracles which contain important clues as to their historicity and the person of Jesus.

I offer this study not as a comprehensive review of the debate about history but as my personal exploration of key questions raised by history and faith.

1

God In History

The Modern Problem

To many Christians the greatest event between the beginning of the church and the present time was the Reformation. But not everyone would agree. If historians were asked to cast their votes to decide which was the most important event, many of them would vote for the Age of Enlightenment. While they would agree that the Reformation left its mark not only on the Protestant and Catholic churches but also on art, culture, and even economic life, they would also say that the world as it is today and our way of thinking about it were more profoundly shaped by the Enlightenment.

The Age of Enlightenment was the age of Rousseau and Voltaire, of Sir Isaac Newton and Edward Gibbon, of David Hume and Thomas Paine, of Benjamin Franklin and Thomas Jefferson, of Gotthold Ephraim Lessing and Immanuel Kant. The Age of Enlightenment saw the American and French revolutions with their philosophies based not on the Word of God but on self-evident truths that were believed to be held by all reasonable people. The German philosopher Immanuel Kant defined enlightenment as

> man's release from his self-incurred tutelage. Tutelage is man's inability to make use of his understanding without direction from another. Self-incurred is this tutelage when its cause lies not in lack of reason but in lack of resolution to use it without direction from another. *Sapere aude!* "Have courage to use your own reason!" — that is the motto of enlightenment.[1]

The eighteenth-century Age of Enlightenment did not come about overnight. Its origins can be traced back to a mood of skepticism that emerged while the Reformation was at its height.[2] It found expression in politics, science, and the study of history no less than in attitudes toward religion. As Kant's definition makes clear, the enlightened mind subjected everything to reason. Accepted beliefs were not to be taken at face value. Traditions were to be tested. Instead of looking for supernatural explanations of nature and history, the natural and the human were the sole factors to be taken into consideration.

Whereas the Reformation was primarily a dispute over Christian doctrine and practice within a commonly accepted Christian world view, the Age of Enlightenment challenged the very basis of that world view. It did so with a combination of arguments and beliefs drawn from science, philosophy, and history. Events that were formerly regarded as acts of God in history were now given natural explanations. Enlightened historians like Conyers Middleton and Edward Gibbon approached their subject with an idea of what was scientifically feasible. If an account of an event did not fit in with that idea, it could safely be relegated to the realm of myth, superstition, and pious belief. In science God ceased to be a term of scientific explanation. The same came to be true of history. Whatever else might be admitted as a term of historical explanation, God and the supernatural could not be allowed that privilege.

For Kant, God was not a personal being but a "regulative principle."[3] It was useful to invoke the notion of God from time to time to give coherence to our understanding of the world, but nothing could really be known about God. To use a phrase that echoes the thought of the twentieth-century philosopher Ludwig Wittgenstein, the notion of God might be said to be "useful nonsense."[4] The modern historian may not be a professed Kantian or Wittgensteinian, but he or she is not apt to use God as a term of historical explanation. Whatever school of thought the historian may belong to, it is no longer respectable to invoke God as a cause of events.

What then are the options before us? Do we have to give up traditional Christian beliefs about God, the Bible, and history? Or do we have to have split minds? Some people find it possible to go to church on Sunday, say the prayers, sing the hymns, and accept everything in terms of the old world view, but for the rest of the week in their secular jobs they think and behave in the realm of the natural and the human. Such an attitude is at best inconsistent and at worst deceptive and lacking in integrity. What is the alternative?

In the rest of this chapter I will sketch the outlines of my approach. Before I do so, I have to confess my conviction that as a Christian I have no business operating with double standards.[5] Because my faith is tied to history, I have to use the best historical tools available for studying history. The rules of the game do not allow me to relax the standards when it comes to matters of faith. I have to look at the pros and cons. I have to weigh arguments. I have to listen to what the state-of-the-art practitioners have to say about the discipline. I might not always accept what they say, but I have to have good reasons for adopting my views rather than theirs. This applies not only to the interpretation of particular events but also to the Christian claim to the right to speak about God in history.

I now turn to three issues. The first of these issues concerns miracles, for miracles present us with a crucial test case. To a modern person steeped in the humanistic and technological culture of the Western world, miracle stories hardly merit serious consideration. They are frequently dismissed as products of the credulous, prescientific world. Scientists and historians are therefore inclined to treat tales of the miraculous as data that tell more about the outlook of other cultures rather than about actual events. To those who think like this, the miracle stories of the Bible are downright incredible. Instead of providing grounds for believing and adopting a theistic view of the world in which God acts in history, they provide good reasons for *not* believing. What are we to make of this argument?

The second issue is Kierkegaard's view of paradox. This has to do with questions like: "How do we think of God's presence in time and space?" "How do we think of God acting in history?" "How could we recognize God's presence?" We may learn something from Kierkegaard as we wrestle with these questions.

The third issue we will look at comes under the heading of "History: Sacred and Secular." The modern secular world wants to give everything a secular interpretation. It insists that all causes in the world are finite causes. It refuses to take at face value Christian claims about God acting in history. How then should the believer respond to this? What grounds do we have for adopting a Christian view of history that proclaims that God acts in history?

Miracles: A Crucial Test Case

To the outsider a great deal of Christianity may not seem to have much directly to do with God. Of course people talk a lot about God, but when they hear or read the word *God*, what they are hearing is a *word* spoken or written by human beings.

The same applies to the Bible. Christians say that it is the Word of God, but outwardly it appears to be a book composed over a period of several centuries, consisting of different kinds of historical documents, all of which were obviously written by human beings. Why then do we say that it is the Word of God? A traditional Christian answer is that it is divinely attested by miracles.[6] Granted that we are not in a position to prove the truth of all the statements in the Bible and granted that in much of it God does not appear directly, nevertheless (the argument goes) the miracles reported in the Bible prove its divine origin. For miracles are supernatural works that only God can perform. If we want examples of this kind of argument, we can find them readily enough in the writings of Calvin, who speaks of miracles confirming, attesting, sealing, and sanctioning the teaching contained in Scripture.[7] In the seventeenth century John Locke described miracles as "the credentials of a messenger delivering a divine religion."[8] He concluded that "where the miracle is admitted, the doctrine cannot be rejected; it comes with the assurance of a divine attestation to him that allows the miracle, and he cannot question its truth."[9]

But this is precisely the problem. Can we really admit miracles? Even before Locke's day people had begun to ask whether they really could believe stories about the miraculous. Locke's contemporary, the Dutch philosopher Benedict Spinoza, was already questioning whether there could be such a thing as a violation of the laws of nature.[10] He argued that "the universal laws of science are decrees of God following from the necessity and perfection of the Divine nature."[11] For God to break his own laws would be "an evident absurdity." Hence, there could be no such thing as a miracle in the accepted sense of the term. Further attacks on miracles came from the pens of the English deists[12] and Conyers Middleton.[13] The attack still heatedly discussed to this day is the one that David Hume launched in section 10 of his *Enquiries Concerning Human Understanding* (1748).[14] We shall look at it shortly, but before we do so it is worth noting that the writers of this period who discussed the subject of miracles were interested in more than the purely theoretical question of whether or not a miracle could occur and what would have to count in order to admit that one had occurred. Skeptics and believers alike had a vested interest. What was at stake was not the abstract possibility of abnormal events but the truth claims that were linked with miracles, for if Calvin, Locke, and other like-minded Christians were right, once the miracle was admitted, the truth claims associated with it followed.

It falls outside the scope of this study to attempt an extensive survey of the miraculous or even to examine detailed evidence for any particular miracle. We shall confine ourselves to two aims: (1) to clarify what is involved in the concept of the miraculous and (2) to ask whether the miraculous and supernatural can legitimately be entertained as history.

a. The concept of miracle. Some say that it is impossible to define miracles. Certainly, if all the factors involved in any alleged instance could be explained, it may be asked what there is to distinguish the miracle from any other event. On the other hand, the New Testament writers regarded certain actions of Jesus, taken in the context of his teaching and Old Testament prophecy, as signs of his relationship with the Father.[15] These signs form an integral part of the New Testament witness. Traditionally, Christians have regarded the biblical miracles as (to use John Locke's phrase) *above reason,* though they were not necessarily *contrary to reason.*[16]

Broadly speaking, miracles fall into two categories. On the one hand there is what has been called the *contingency concept* or *coincidence concept*[17] of miracle. In this case there is no apparent violation of the laws of nature but a conjunction of circumstances that is so unexpected and improbable according to the expected course of events and so beneficial to at least one of the parties involved that some would see in it a supernatural ordering of circumstances. A case in point would be the "miracle" of Dunkirk when against all odds the British army in World War II escaped from being trapped by Hitler's overwhelming forces. On the level of natural explanation this escape could be put down to unexpected weather conditions and the failure of the German high command to press home their advantage.

Another instance would be that of a child playing with his or her pedal car on an unattended railroad crossing, heedless of the approach of an express which stops suddenly for a reason unconnected with the child.[18] Some of the biblical signs might come under this category. It would not detract from their significance if we saw in some of the healings psychosomatic factors[19] or if we attributed the temporary drying up of the Red Sea to the "strong east wind" that blew all night.[20]

In such cases it is possible to suggest a historical explanation in terms of medical, natural, scientific, or other factors. We are in the realm of natural phenomena. A religious person might see in it the work of Providence, because he sees it in the framework of belief. An unbeliever might attribute it to extraordinary luck, because he is inclined to see things in the framework of chance or superstition. But it is also possible that a previously uncommitted person might see in it some indication of a higher ordering of events. It is not that a divine agency has directly intervened, suspending ordinary causes and the laws of nature; rather, the circumstances and conjunction of ordinary causes make the event unique.

But not all miracles seem to fall into this category. Many of the major signs of the New Testament appear to be *violations of the law of nature*. With R. F. Holland we may say that this *violation concept* of miracle involves "two incompatible things: (1) that it is impossible and (2) that it has happened."[21]

> A miracle, though it cannot only be this, must at least be something the occurrence of which can be categorized at one and the same time as empirically certain and conceptually impossible. If it were less than conceptually impossible it would reduce merely to a very unusual occurrence such as could be treated (because of the empirical certainty) in the manner of a decisive experiment and result in a modification to the prevailing conception of natural law; while if it were less than empirically certain nothing more would be called for in regard to it than a suspension of judgment.[22]

There are two main lines of objection to this—one philosophical and logical and the other historical. The philosophical objection asks whether this concept of miracle is not self-contradictory and thus nonsensical in the same way that the notions of a round square or a female father are self-contradictory and nonsensical. The answer is that there is *more than one kind of conceptual impossibility*. The founding fathers of America could not have conceived how it would be possible for someone to watch a screen in London and see events taking place in the New World (and still less on the moon) as they actually happen. Nowadays even children know that such occurrences are possible by television satellite.

It may be objected that such events are not miracles in the strict sense of the term, in that they are now recurrent and are capable of being explained by modern science. However, the concept of miracle I defend here does not necessarily preclude eventual explanation. It is not part of the Christian concept of a miracle to say that God could not use natural means in order to bring the event about. To recognize such means does not make a case of healing any less miraculous. If we are able to see an explanation in terms of the natural order, an event which might previously have been thought of as an instance of the violation concept of miracle would turn out to be an instance of the contingency concept of miracle. This approach to miracles does not rest on a vague appeal to the principle of indeterminacy in physics.[23] It would not help the believer to say that miracles were the result of the random behavior of atomic particles. For that would mean that miracles were random flukes of nature and not the purposeful, gracious action of God.

Nor does the believer have to say that miracles are unique, unrepeatable events. They may be rare and not repeatable in the same way that daily occurrences like the rising and setting of the sun is repeatable. But it is not part of the Christian concept of miracle to say that the same miracle could not happen twice. Even though the resurrection of Jesus was unique, it is presented in the New Testament as the ground of the believer's hope in the afterlife. The traditional Christian belief in resurrection involves belief that we shall be raised like Christ.[24] The sign-like character of the New Testament miracles is just as important as their inexplicability.[25] Indeed, the former remains even when a conceivable explanation has been found. What I am contending for is the legitimacy of believing in what to us at present is unique and conceptually impossible, provided that there are adequate reasons for doing so. And this leads us to the question of whether the miraculous and supernatural can legitimately be entertained as history.

b. The legitimacy of the miraculous and supernatural in history. David Hume defined miracle as "a transgression of a law of nature by a particular volition of the Deity or by the interposition of some invisible agent."[26] His argument fell into two parts. The first part of the argument claimed that "a miracle is a violation of the laws of nature; and as a firm and unalterable experience has established these laws, the proof against a miracle, from the very nature of the fact, is as entire as any argument from experience can possibly be imagined."[27]

The second part of Hume's argument noted four further lines of objection. All four lines had to do with the *nature* of the evidence for miracles.

1. The first line of argument claimed that miracles generally lack competent witnesses.

> There is not to be found, in all history, any miracle attested by a sufficient number of men, of such unquestioned good-sense, education, and learning, as to secure us against all delusion in themselves; of such undoubted integrity, as to place them beyond all suspicion of any design to deceive others; of such credit and reputation in the eyes of mankind, as to have a great deal to lose in case of their being detected in any falsehood; and at the same time,

attesting facts performed in such a public manner and in so celebrated a part of the world, as to render the detection unavoidable: All which circumstances are requisite to give us a full assurance on the testimony of men.[28]

2. The second line of argument drew attention to a common failing of human nature: love of gossip and the tendency to enlarge upon the truth. Enthusiasts for religion are not unknown to perpetrate falsehoods "with the best intentions in the world, for the sake of promoting so holy a cause."[29]

3. Third, Hume observed that miracles "are observed chiefly to abound among ignorant and barbarous nations," and where they are admitted among civilized people they will be found to have been received "from ignorant and barbarous ancestors, who transmitted them with that inviolable sanction and authority, which always attend received opinions."[30]

4. Hume's crowning argument was that the miracles of rival religions cancel each other out.[31] The claim to miracles by rival religions means that they cannot be used to establish the truth of any given religion.[32] From all this Hume concluded that, if miracles are to be accepted at all, they are to be accepted on the basis of faith. In reaching this conclusion, Hume inverted the traditional approach exemplified by Locke, but at the same time made it clear that any faith that accepted miracles was a groundless faith.[33]

The plausibility of Hume's case owes not a little to the fact that many alleged instances of the miraculous are open to his objections. But it may be asked whether his sweeping criticisms are not in fact too wholesale. We take first the four lines of objection in the second part of his argument. If objection 1 were applied rigorously, it would preclude not only the miraculous but also the possibility of accepting as historical almost everything that happened outside the urban centers of western Europe prior to the sixteenth century. Even so, it may be asked whether Hume would be willing to accept testimony to the miraculous on such a basis. For he went on to admit instances of miracles wrought in France in modern times which "were immediately proved upon the spot, before judges of unquestioned integrity, attested by witnesses of credit and distinction, in a learned age, and on the most eminent theater that is now in the world."[34] Nevertheless, Hume refused to credit such testimony on the grounds of "the absolute impossibility or miraculous nature of the events, which they relate."[35] In other words, no amount of historical testimony would suffice. With this point we are brought back to Hume's major argument, that miracles are violations of the laws of nature and as such are impossible.

With regard to objection 2 it has been pointed out that not all people are credulous and gullible with a natural penchant for embroidering the truth. Plenty of people are natural skeptics. As a general criterion for assessing testimony to the unusual and miraculous, Hume's argument as it stands will not do. In assessing any given testimony, we have to assess the character and motivation of the testifier. As Richard Swinburne has aptly remarked, "How many people are in each group, and in which group are the witnesses to any alleged miracle are matters for particular historical investigation."[36]

Objection 3 is as imprecise as objection 1 and is open to similar criticism. It is absurd to demand as a test of historicity that those who testify to an event should subscribe to the same metaphysical beliefs and world view as oneself. Moreover, the argument does not distinguish sufficiently between the testimony to any given event and the explanation that the witnesses to the event may or may not offer. We may be competent to revise the latter in the light of superior understanding, but the validity of the testimony *that* a given event happened depends rather on the honesty of the witnesses, their capacity not to be deceived, and their proximity to the event. Nor does Hume's argument take into account other forms of evidence, such as physical traces and changed behavior patterns that may be connected with events.[37]

Hume's objection 4 also has less substance than might appear at first sight. Swinburne has commented:

> In fact evidence for a miracle "wrought in one religion" is only evidence against the occurrence of a miracle "wrought in another religion" if the two miracles, if they occurred, would be evidence for propositions of the two religious systems incompatible with each other. It is hard to think of pairs of alleged miracles of this type. If there were evidence for a Roman Catholic miracle which was evidence for the doctrine of transubstantiation and evidence for a Protestant miracle which was evidence against it, here we could have a case of the conflict of evidence which Hume claims occurs generally with alleged miracles. . . . But . . . most alleged miracles do not give rise to conflicts of this kind. Most alleged miracles, if they occurred as reported, would show at most the power of a god or gods and their concern for the needs of men, and little more specific in the way of doctrine. A miracle wrought in the context of the Hindu religion and one wrought in the context of the Christian religion will not in general tend to show that specific details of their systems are true, but, at most, that there is a god concerned with

the needs of those who worship, which is a proposition accepted in both systems.[38]

We might add that the New Testament writers never claim that God shows goodness only to those who share their doctrines.[39] On the other hand, they do recognize that people habitually persist in defective notions of God when they ought to have known better. Reflection on natural phenomena around them, Paul argued, ought to have been sufficient to show people that God should not be thought of as a thing or an animal.[40] The healing of a lame man should have been seen by the inhabitants of Lystra in the context of "a living God who made the heaven and the earth and the sea and all that is in them."[41] Instead, the populace jumped to the conclusion that "the gods have come to us in the likeness of men." Barnabas they called Zeus, the chief god (because he remained silent), and Paul they called Hermes, the messenger of the gods (because he was doing most of the talking).

Like any other occurrence, any event of this kind is open to different interpretations. As a sheer matter of fact, people often remain content with whatever interpretation they put on the event. It is not that the event in itself is necessarily ambiguous and that there are no indications in its context as to its significance. Rather, historical events (like natural phenomena) have a significance that does not always lie on the surface. They challenge us to reflect on their meaning. If we come to something with entrenched opinions, we can very easily stick with our opinions and treat the thing accordingly, but in sticking to our preconceived ideas we might miss the whole point. On the other hand, there might be something in an event or in the report of an event that challenges our preconceptions and the way we look at things. The miracle stories of the New Testament, especially the Easter message of the resurrection of Jesus, are prime examples of this very point.

In the last analysis, Hume's decisive argument is his first and major one, that miracles are contrary to the established laws of nature, and therefore no amount of testimony will suffice as proof of their factuality. As Hume recognized, natural laws are statistical, and their predictive character is based on past observation.[42] As such, they are open to correction and modification. The force of any given formulation depends on the degree of its corroboration.

We may grant that whatever can be explained is not a violation of law[43] and that any *established* violation of a given law would simply show that the law has been inadequately formulated.[44] We would thus be back with the contingency concept of miracle. Nevertheless, such an event would still retain its sign-like character in its historical context.[45] The crucial question that Hume raises, however, is: Are we justified in accepting testimony to an event that has no obvious parallel in our experience, especially when it rests on the word of one or two witnesses who may not even be eyewitnesses?

We shall return to the question of assessing evidence, and in particular to the question of assessing this kind of testimony, in chapter 2, "Rules, Principles, and Explanations." In the meantime we shall notice two lines of thought that have a bearing on this subject and have been put forward by Richard Swinburne and Alan Richardson.

Swinburne observes that such evidence as is currently available about the occurrence of violations and the circumstances of their occurrence is not on balance strong enough to render very probable the existence of a divine agency that intervenes in human affairs. The case is radically different, however, if we have evidence of other types for or against the existence and character of God.[46] Such evidence (as in the natural sciences) would be cumulative and may derive from reflection on nature, on providence, on history, on the testimony of Scripture, and on personal experience. As such, its validity and relevance will itself be the subject of appropriate investigation. What is important, however, is to notice the general shape of the argument. The value of particular arguments of pieces of evidence is affected by our overall view of their possibility, probability, or feasibility.

> If any of these arguments have any weight, we would need only slender historical evidence of certain miracles to have reasonable grounds to believe in their occurrence, just as we need only slender historical evidence to have reasonable grounds for belief in the occurrence of events whose occurrence is rendered probable by natural laws. We take natural laws to show the improbability of violations thereof because they are well-established parts of our overall view of how the world works. But if they are relevant for that reason, then so is any other part of our overall view of how the world works. And if from our study of its operation we conclude that we have evidence for the existence of a God of such a character as to be liable to intervene in the natural order under certain circumstances, the overall world-view gives not a high prior improbability, but a high prior probability to the occurrence of miracles under those circumstances.[47]

Swinburne's approach to the question turns, therefore, on the general presuppositions that we bring to each particular case. It leaves open the question of what are the ultimate grounds on which one can base belief, but on his premises they cannot include the miraculous, for whether one accepts the miraculous depends in part on precisely these grounds. This is not to say that the miraculous could play no part at all in shaping one's view of God, any more than one would say that a scientific hypothesis that is dependent on the validity of other hypotheses cannot yield valid insights into the nature of things. But as such, it cannot serve as the ultimate basis for belief. This should not worry the believer, as the biblical writers never seem to have viewed miraculous signs as an ultimate basis for belief. Rather, the signs point beyond themselves to the significance of certain events and people *within* the given context of belief in God.

We shall look more closely in the next chapter at Alan Richardson's use of the concept of hypothesis in historical explanation. For now, I would like to note how Richardson applies it specifically to the question of the resurrection of Jesus. What are we to make of the New Testament belief in the resurrection of Jesus? There are three possible types of explanation here. The first is that it happened in some sense as a historical fact. We need not be able to say precisely how it happened, any more than historians are able to say how Hannibal achieved the feat of crossing the Alps complete with elephants, cavalry, and a large army. The historian need not be able to reconstruct in detail how the things he accepts as fact happened. Nor need he be able to observe the events in question. In fact, the historian is never an observer of events unless he or she happens to have been a personal eyewitness. Historical "facts" are inferences from pieces of testimony and other evidence the historian has good reason to accept.

The second alternative is that the claim that Jesus was raised was deliberately fraudulent. Richardson rejects this on the grounds that "it is incredible that a faith which brought reconciliation with the all-holy God and peace and charity amongst men could have originated in a fraudulent conspiracy."[48]

The third possible explanation is that the disciples were mistaken. This view involves dismissal of the claims of the first disciples to have found that the tomb was empty and to have encountered the risen Christ,[49] and it also involves devising a different explanation from the one given by the first Christians for the origin of the church.

Against those latter alternatives Richardson puts the view that "either Christ's resurrection called the Church's faith into being or we must give some more rationally coherent account of how that faith with all its tremendous consequences arose."[50] He cannot remain content with Günther Bornkamm's view that "the last historical fact" available to scholars is "the Easter faith of the first disciples."[51] Underlying such a view is the implicit contention that the historian can deal with questions such as "Did the disciples believe that God raised Jesus from the dead?" (since this involves purely human terms) but not with a question such as "Did God raise Jesus from the dead?" (since this involves the metaphysical and supernatural). Richardson insists that Bornkamm's

> attitude involves the abandoning of historical method altogether, for the historian cannot admit that there are any "last facts" in history, for they would be causeless events. . . . History is a causal nexus in which there can be no breaks, no events which are in principle inexplicable. The historian, if he is to be true to his calling, is bound to go on to consider the various possible explanations of the alleged happening or, if he can, to find a new and better one.[52]

It is not a question of how Jesus was raised or whether he had a "spiritual" or a "physical" body, since in our present state of knowledge we know so little about "spirits" and "bodies."[53] But that Jesus was raised is for Richardson the hypothesis that explains the available data.

Richardson (like Swinburne) holds that an element of faith is involved in such a judgment. It may be observed that he is using "faith" not necessarily in the sense of commitment and trust, but in the sense of settled convictions about God and the world.[54] It may be asked whether such a predisposing faith is a necessary condition. Does Richardson's approach require it? Did the first Christians approach the resurrection with such a prerequisite faith? In both cases the answer would seem to be in the negative. On the one hand, a hypothesis can be entertained as an explanation without any special commitment other than a willingness to see whether it fits the case. The case itself determines whether the hypothesis is adequate. On the other hand, it would seem that the event the first Christians least expected was the resurrection of Jesus. It was encounter with the risen Christ that awakened faith, not faith that created resurrection belief.[55]

Kierkegaard's Paradox

At this point in the argument I would like to do something that might look like a detour. What is more, it might appear to some like a dangerous detour into irrationalism. I want to introduce a line of argument drawn from the nineteenth-century Danish writer Søren Kierkegaard. Kierkegaard is widely credited with being the grandfather of secular existentialism. Those who see him through the eyes of Francis Schaeffer will judge Kierkegaard's talk about the "leap of faith" and "the absurd" as a leap into irrationalism and despair.[56] To them Kierkegaard must be avoided at all costs except as a cautionary example of what *not* to do. Moreover, it might not appear to be altogether relevant to bring Kierkegaard in at this point. After all, he was not a historian. He described himself as a kind of poet. In many of his writings he used pseudonyms, and it is not always easy to grasp what he is driving at.[57] When certain statements are taken at face value and out of context, it certainly looks as if Kierkegaard is the advocate of an extremely skeptical attitude to history in general and to Christian origins in particular. On top of that, it looks as if he is saying that such skepticism does not matter. In fact, it even seems to be an advantage.

A case in point is the oft-quoted passage from Kierkegaard's *Philosophical Fragments* concerning the first generation of Christians:

> Even if the contemporary generation had not left anything behind except these words, "We have believed that in such and such a year the god appeared in the humble form of a servant, lived and taught among us, and then died"—this is more than enough. The contemporary generation would have done what is needful for this little announcement, this world-historical *nota bene*, is enough to become an occasion for someone who comes later, and the most prolix report can never in all eternity become more for the person who comes later.[58]

It looks as if Kierkegaard is saying here that history does not matter much; what counts is how you react and what you believe.

This can very easily lead to a *Wizard of Oz* situation. In L. Frank Baum's modern American fairy story the straw man, the tin man, the cowardly lion, and little Dorothy go off in search of the famous wizard who, they believe, will help them get what they want most—a brain, a heart, courage, and the security of home. Unfortunately, when they find him, the wizard turns out to be an ordinary man with no miraculous powers, but the companions then realize that in the course of their adventures they have acquired by themselves the things that they thought could be given to them only supernaturally. Well, there is a moral in all this. But is there no more than this to Christianity? And is this the kind of religion that Kierkegaard really had in mind?

As in all things, it is dangerous to take statements out of context. It is doubly so with Kierkegaard, for if we study Kierkegaard in his own words (as distinct from what people have said that he said), the picture that emerges is not that of the incipient skeptical existentialist philosopher but of a deeply committed Christian. If labels are to be attached to him, it might be more accurate to describe him as a dialectical theologian[59] with a fairly conservative (indeed, uncritical) approach to history. Basic to Kierkegaard's whole outlook (as it is to the biblical writers) is the thought that God is *other*. The significant point is the way in which Kierkegaard develops the idea. God exists on a different plane and in a different way from ourselves. As he put it in one of his *Christian Discourses*, "If the difference is infinite between God who is in heaven and thee who art on earth, the difference is infinitely greater between the holy One and the sinner."[60]

There is both a metaphysical and a moral distinction here. It expresses the fundamental disjunction between God and the world that underlies Kierkegaard's entire thought. This disjunction is radical and complete. It cannot be overcome on man's side, but it is overcome on God's. How? Kierkegaard explains this by invoking the notions of *paradox* and even *absolute paradox*. Finite reason can grasp only what is finite and rational. It cannot, therefore, grasp God. Pardoxically, even to obtain the knowledge that God is unlike him, man needs the help of God.[61] The gulf between man and God is bridged from God's side supremely in the Incarnation. Thus, in the *Philosophical Fragments*, Kierkegaard's pseudonymous author, Johannes Climacus, put forward the suggestion that, in order to be man's teacher, "the god"

> wanted to be on the basis of equality with the single individual so that he could completely understand him. Thus the paradox becomes even more terrible, or the same paradox has the duplexity by which it manifests itself as the absolute—negatively, by bringing into prominence the absolute difference of sins and, positively, by wanting to annul this absolute difference in the absolute equality.[62]

We need to notice what is involved here. Johannes Climacus is speaking hypothetically about what would have to happen if human beings were to know God. Speaking hypothetically, therefore, he talks about "the god." As the argument develops, it turns out that what would have to happen is amazingly like

what the Christian story claims to have actually happened.[63]
We must not allow ourselves to get sidetracked by following the
ramifications of Kierkegaard's argument. For our present
purposes we need simply to grasp the main point about God in
history.

Not only is God absolutely unlike us human beings, but in
the Incarnation as our teacher God is absolutely *like* one of us.
This means that in Christ—as in nature[64]—God is *incognito.*
What people saw when they saw Jesus was a human being.
What they heard when they listened to his words were human
words. Even when they saw Jesus healing someone or casting
out a demon, they did not see God *directly.* In scene 1 they
might have seen a deranged man accost Jesus. In scene 2 they
might have heard Jesus saying something to the man and the
man beginning to behave differently. In scene 3 they were, as
Mark tells us, "all amazed, so that they questioned among
themselves, saying, 'What is this? A new teaching! With
authority he commands even the unclean spirits, and they obey
him'" (Mark 1:27 RSV). What they did not—and could not
possibly—see with their human senses was the presence of the
transcendent God.

In other words, from a purely physical point of view, what
people could see with their senses was something human and
finite. The crucial question is: "What should they make of it?"
"What construction should they put on it?" From a strictly
rational standpoint the paradox that Jesus is God incarnate is
"absurd."[65] The notion is incomprehensible and self-contradictory. From the purely formal standpoint of logic it could
therefore be said that Christianity involves faith in the absurd.
Or, to put it the other way around, the object of Christian faith
calls in question our rational capacities.

Kierkegaard's thought is taken a step further in those
passages where Kierkegaard speaks of being contemporary
with Christ. To be a contemporary with Christ is not for
Kierkegaard a matter of living at the same time as Jesus in close
physical proximity with him. At best this is a matter of being a
contemporary with him only on the level of time. What really
matters is to be a contemporary with him on the level of
eternity. The real contemporary is the one who transcends the
limitations of time by perceiving the eternal in the temporal. For
on the plane of time and space the eternal is hidden. In a later
work, *Training in Christianity*, Kierkegaard puts it like this:

It was Christ's free will and determination from all eternity to be
incognito. So when people think to do Him honour by saying or

thinking, "If I had been contemporary with Him, I should have known Him directly," they really insult Him, and since it is Christ they insult, this means that they are blasphemous. . . . Oh, loftiest height of self-abnegation when the incognito succeeds so well that even if He were inclined to speak directly no one would believe Him. . . .And now in the case of the God-Man! He is God, but chooses to become the individual man. This, as we have seen, is the profoundest incognito, or the most impenetrable unrecognizableness that is possible; for the contradiction between being God and being an individual man is the greatest possible, the infinitely qualitative contradiction.[66]

In his private papers Kierkegaard expressed the point geometrically: "Christ veritably relates tangentially to the earth (the divine cannot relate in any other way); He has no place where to lay his head. A tangent is a straight line which touches the circle at only one single point."[67] The conclusion to be drawn from this position is that there is no "direct communication" between man and God. To be directly recognizable is the mark of an idol. The God man—which is Kierkegaard's term for expressing the reality of Jesus Christ—is known only as "the object of faith." "Direct recognizableness is paganism."[68]

In making these points, Kierkegaard is saying more than Lessing in his dictum that the accidental truths of history can never become the proof of the necessary truths of reason. Lessing was concerned with the uncertainty of historical assertions that lack the compulsion of self-evident truth. Kierkegaard was concerned with the question of God in history. For him it was not a matter of evidential or logical certainty. Faith in God involves a realm that transcends evidence and logic, but this does not make Kierkegaard a radical in the modern sense of the term. Although he called his *Concluding Unscientific Postscript to the Philosophical Fragments* "An Existential Contribution," he had no desire to reduce the gospel to existential self-awareness. He was certainly concerned with the elements of choice and decision in man's apprehension of reality. But Kierkegaard's scheme of reality was not one of purely immanent structures. Indeed, it could be said that his primary concern was to recognize and express what was involved in believing in the transcendent God who acts in history. Moreover, he was doing this in the face of idealist philosophy and contemporary churchmanship which were dominated by immanentism.

Nor was Kierkegaard skeptical about the historical authenticity of the biblical records. Although he was acutely aware of what was going on in the intellectual world, his writings betray a profound lack of interest in the critical debates of his time. In both his philosophical and devotional writings he consistently takes Scripture at its face value. The quotation about a minimal belief, with which we began this discussion of Kierkegaard, comes in the context of a discussion not of critical history but of the relationship between the temporal and the eternal. The text goes on to say:

> If we wish to state in the briefest possible way the relation of a contemporary to someone who comes later—without, however, sacrificing correctness for brevity—then we can say: *By means of* the contemporary's report (the occasion), the person who comes later believes by virtue of the condition he himself receives from the god. —The contemporary's report is the occasion for the one who comes later, just as immediate contemporaneity is the occasion for the contemporary, and if the report is what it ought to be (a believer's report), it will then occasion the same ambiguity of awareness that he himself had, occasioned by immediate contemporaneity.[69]

Again we must stress that the writer here, Johannes Climacus, is speaking formally and hypothetically about the conditions that would apply if a being such as a god were to communicate with human beings in history by becoming a human being himself. History is the *occasion* for the encounter. Such an encounter, however, involves more than outward actions even though it is the outward actions that are seen by the senses. When someone tries to communicate what happened, he or she can describe only the outward actions. Even on a purely human level we would need discernment in order to interpret the significance of the actions. But this too has to be communicated in human terms. In the case of God's action in the Incarnation, Matthew's gospel makes it clear that discernment is a gift of God.[70] What can be communicated historically is human testimony. Insight into God's presence and working is a gift from God himself.

To some of Kierkegaard's readers this defense of God's presence in the world, in Christ, and in history has seemed a Pyrrhic victory: he has won the battle but at enormous cost. Kierkegaard seems to come perilously close to saying that God is there but that he is unknowable. However, I do not think that this is Kierkegaard's position. Certainly he is saying that God remains transcendent even in his revelation. What can be seen are the effects but not the cause. In the effects God remains hidden and *incognito*, but this is not the same as saying that he is unknowable. Rather, God may be known through the effects in faith. This can only be done by the individual as the individual responds in faith.

In a sense, Kierkegaard's approach is like a sacramental approach to reality. The sacramental matter—the bread, the wine, and the water—is not transformed into something other than what it is. It remains whatever it is. But it becomes the material means of encountering God. If we look at it from a purely material point of view, all that we can see will be matter; but if we use the sacrament in faith, in the context of the belief system of the Christian faith, the sacrament becomes the means of God's gracious dealing with us. The same might be said of the Bible. Outwardly it looks like any other book. It is written in human language by human authors. It is printed on paper by machines using ink. Where then is the divine aspect of it? Why do Christians say that it is the Word of God? The answer is that God speaks to them in it.

Now all this may look like a circular argument and nothing more than an elaborate attempt to cover up the fact that religious belief is a matter of blind faith that pays no regard to facts. The difficulties may be stated in various ways, but they come back to the same point. If God is so hidden, even in the supreme event of revelation, which for Christians is the coming of Jesus Christ into the world, it seems perfectly possible to give an account of nature and history (including gospel history) without reference to God. If so, why do we need to bring God into it at all? Indeed, have we any right to bring God into it? Are there any grounds for a "Christian" interpretation of history? It seems but half a step from Kierkegaardian interpretation of reality in which the transcendence of God is fundamental, but hidden, to an atheistic, existential one that does without God altogether.

History: Sacred and Secular

Kierkegaard's standpoint and that of the secularist are like the two sides of the same coin. In both cases only the finite is directly observed. But this is not the same as saying that all events have to be understood *exclusively* in secular terms. Nor does it mean that we shall *automatically* adopt a skeptical outlook on everything.[71] The historian may take a high view of the historicity of some accounts and documents and a low view of others, depending on his evaluation of the evidence. We may even (like the secular historian) be predisposed to accept the historicity of some accounts and not of others. Such a predisposition may be perfectly proper in the same sense in which a jury may be properly predisposed to accept the testimony of one witness and to reject that of another on the grounds that there is reason to believe that one witness is competent and trustworthy whereas the other is not.

We shall return to these questions later on. In the meantime it is important to notice that a good deal can be said for Kierkegaard's approach. When we look at history—including our own personal histories and biblical history—it can be described continuously in finite, not to say secular, terms. We might instance the crossing of the Red Sea, the entry into Canaan, the message of the prophets, the fall of Jerusalem and the Exile, much of the teaching of Jesus, or Paul's missionary journeys. When we look back at "God's hand" in our lives, we see a succession of events that are *isomorphic* with those of the rest of humankind—that is, they have the same sort of form and structure. Believers experience joy and sorrow. They know success and failure. They go through the same human cycle from birth to the grave. In Christian experience we do not suddenly find a suspension of natural, social, economic, and historical causes. They are all continuously present in our daily lives. We do not experience the direct, pure presence of God. It is always mediated through something, perhaps through reading the Bible or in prayer. We may experience what we believe to be the presence of God in worship or some event in our lives, but it is always mediated through something or someone. In normal experience we do not encounter God directly, as he is in himself.

The same was true of the personalities in the Bible in their normal experience. We may leave aside as possible exceptions such experiences as Isaiah's vision in the temple,[72] the transfiguration of Jesus,[73] the encounters of the disciples with the risen Christ,[74] Paul's account of being caught up into "the third heaven,"[75] and John's vision on Patmos.[76] It is not that these are unimportant but that they are unique events, involving factors not present in normal biblical experience. Direct encounter with God was not part of normal experience even in biblical times. But indirect encounters with God, as mediated through God's Word, through history, through worship, and through the whole range of experience was part of their way of life. And this has been the experience of believers down through the ages.

While we live in the flesh in time and space we are not able to see directly the One who is not subject to time and space. Moses was told that no one could see God's face and live.[77] In the Sermon on the Mount Jesus declared that seeing God was something promised to the pure in heart.[78] The apostle Paul had to remind the Corinthians that "now we see but a poor reflection; then we shall see face to face. Now I know in part; then I shall know fully, even as I am fully known."[79] The same is true of our own experience. We may say things like: "feeling the hand of God upon us," "receiving an anointing from the Spirit," and "knowing the peace of God which passes all understanding," but it is always contained in this or that event or experience and is apprehended in ways capable of being described and analyzed by those competent in such fields as psychology and neuroscience.

Why then do we give to our experiences a religious interpretation and attribute some things to God and perhaps other things to Satan? Is it just a matter of habit or social behavior? Do we have any legitimate justification for giving our experiences a religious interpretation? One of the reasons why we do so is that we use history as a paradigm for interpretation. A paradigm is just another word for a typical example, an archetype, something that can be used as a pattern. A paradigm in a book on grammar or a textbook on a foreign language shows how words are used in their various forms. In taking a paradigm from history, we are using an event, a situation, a person, a saying, etc. in order to help us understand and interpret our own situation. Paradigms serve as presuppositions for our understanding and as models for our interpretation of other events and experiences. They may be psalms, parables, pronouncements, or incidents. We identify ourselves and our situations with them. What was previously a hard or confused situation is seen by the believer in a different light. It is not that he has had a *direct* experience of God in it, but he has gained a new perspective and with it an indirect apprehension of God.

But if this is all there is to it, are we not open to the charges of fideism, primitive prescientific thinking, and naïve believism? The answer to this will turn partly on whether what we are doing is *reading into* both past and present factors which are not really there or whether we are genuinely *reading them out of* parallel situations.[80] It will also turn on whether we have good grounds for belief in God and for the kind of God we believe in. We may have certain arguments from the natural world. If so, we must show that these hold good not only for a God of nature but also for the God of history. It may be that in some of our interpretations of history God is presupposed. That is, he is not seen directly, nor does he figure as one actor alongside of the other actors. On the other hand, our account of the given situation would be incomplete without God.

In their very different ways Francis Schaeffer[81] and Alan Richardson[82] see the Christian faith as involving an element of presupposition. They see the Christian interpretation of history as an explanation or hypothesis. Schaeffer's apologetic charges the atheistic and agnostic view of the world with irrationalism and presents a biblical, theistic view of God and the world as a radical alternative which alone is able to give coherence and meaning to history. God is a metaphysical, moral, and epistemological necessity. Only by adopting this explanation of the world and history can humans be saved from relapsing into meaninglessness and despair. Schaeffer's approach involves a confrontation of world views in which the Christian one is vindicated by its ability to make sense of the universe. The Christian is justified in introducing God into his account of history and experience when occasion warrants it, because God is warranted by his general frame of reference.

Richardson's approach is more directly concerned with history itself. For him, biblical theology involves "the framing of an hypothesis concerning the content and character of the faith of the apostolic Church, and the testing of this hypothesis in the light of all available techniques of New Testament scholarship, historical, critical, literary, philological, archaeological, and so on."[83] It thus involves recognition that biblical events are capable of explanation in terms of these various scientific disciplines. But it also involves an element of faith on the part of the investigator.[84] It is "scientific" in the same way that any other science is scientific. The scientist never starts with an empty mind. He does not go around collecting facts in the expectation that when he has discovered enough of them he will find that they conform to an orderly pattern of law. The reverse is the truth. The scientist gets a hunch, frames a hypothesis, and then devises experiments to see whether the observable data can be seen better in this new way.

A Newton or an Einstein has a hunch about a wider uniformity in the behavior of falling apples or revolving planets. Its verification lies in devising means of testing the hypothesis. There are obvious limitations to the parallel of the scientist and the historian,[85] but in both cases an explanation or hypothesis is validated by its capacity to account for something in a way which takes into account the relevant facts and which also accords with the body of accepted truth. Its rivals are excluded by their failure to do this in one or another respect. Thus Richardson defends the "hypothesis" that

Jesus himself is the author of the brilliant re-interpretation of the Old Testament scheme of salvation ("Old Testament theology") which is found in the New Testament, and that the events of the life, "signs," passion and resurrection of Jesus, as attested by the apostolic witness, can account for the "data" of the New Testament better than any other hypothesis current today. It makes better "sense," or better history, than, for instance the hypothesis that St. Paul (or someone else) transformed the simple ethical monotheism of a young Jewish carpenter-rabbi into a new mystery-religion of the dying-and-rising god pattern with the crucified rabbi as its cult-hero.[86]

The contention here is that the "religious," theistic interpretation of Jesus does not mean that we must ignore the social, economic, political, and other secular factors in his history. They are valid on their particular level, and an adequate understanding of Jesus requires them. Richardson's contention is that the history itself contains elements that point beyond these factors and that these elements can best be accounted for on the hypothesis that they represent valid aspects of reality. Conversely, the hypothesis that the world is a closed system of finite causes that preclude the notions of God and of the supernatural means that these elements have to be ignored or explained away in a manner that does violence to the data at our disposal.

In dealing with history, we are dealing with more than reports from the past about the past. We are not dealing simply with the detritus of the past, the loose mass of historical remains that have come down to us in the present. Everything that comes to us has to be interpreted and evaluated. We can do this only by using presuppositions, paradigms, and hypotheses, which are in turn shown to be useful or useless by their adequacy to deal with the material in hand. Frequently, a hypothesis will have to be corrected and supplemented by further hypotheses. When a whole way of looking at something has to be revised, there occurs a "paradigm shift."[87] In science a "paradigm shift" occurred when Newtonian physics began to be supplemented by Einstein's theory of relativity. It was not that everything that Newton discovered was shown to be wrong; rather, it was that the new physics required new ways of looking at reality. The old ways had to be supplemented and corrected by the new.

The view that I am arguing for in this book is that reality is too complex to be handled simply in terms of one set of hypotheses or paradigms or in a single, unified world view. The world view of modern science needs to be supplemented by the perspectives afforded us by God's action in history. We need to work with as many hypotheses and paradigms as God's reality requires in order to gain understanding.

To make these points is not to dispose of all problems at a single stroke. Whether any given hypothesis or paradigm is appropriate depends on detailed investigation of the data available. But to make these points is to indicate the general shape of the question and the kind of argument it involves.

2

Rules, Principles, and Explanations

We cannot get away from history any more than a fish swimming in the sea can get away from the water. Human beings live in history. History no less than nature forms our environment. Things that happened in the past affect the course of the present. Our attitudes toward history—conscious or unconscious, naïve or sophisticated—shape the way we view things. For the Christian believer questions like "Did Jesus really say and do the things that the Gospels say he did?" are of great importance. The same sort of question could be asked about Abraham Lincoln, Napoleon Bonaparte, Queen Elizabeth I, Joan of Arc—or about anybody. Did they really do and say the things they are said to have done? How do we know that the reports we have about them are truthful? Do we accept things just because other people happen to believe them? How does the historian decide?

The historian's questions do not stop there. The historian is concerned about more than settling questions like the correct dates of events, the number of people present on any given occasion, and who said what to whom. To operate on this level is to operate on the level of the chronicler. The historian cannot operate without asking such questions, but more important are questions about causes, meaning, significance, and interpretation.

The problem is doubly acute for the religious believer, for the believer has to face up to the question of whether there should be double standards. Should one set of standards apply to ordinary history and another set to religious history? My own view is that the same general standards that apply to ordinary history should apply to questions of religious history. I say this for two reasons. First, I believe that if an event is historical it is accessible by whatever means are appropriate for understand-

ing it. Second, I would have a nagging feeling that my faith
would be undermined if it could not stand up to rigorous
scrutiny. How then do historians go about dealing with
history?

Art, Craft, or Science?

The debate about whether history is an art, a craft, or a
science is at least as old as the present century and will
probably continue for a long time. I do not propose to attempt
to settle it here. However, I would like to take as a text for this
section the pronouncement of R. G. Collingwood that

> history has this in common with every other science: that the
> historian is not allowed to claim any single piece of knowledge,
> except where he can justify his claim by exhibiting to himself in the
> first place, and secondly to anyone else who is both able and willing
> to follow his demonstrations, the grounds upon which it is based.[1]

Van Austin Harvey has remarked that philosophers of history
tend to divide into two groups:

> (1) those who have maintained that entitlement to credence is
> directly proportionate to the degree to which historical explanations
> approximate to scientific explanations; and (2) those who have
> argued that historical explanations are of a unique sort and require
> no reference whatever to the hallmark of scientific explanations, the
> subsumption of a statement under a law.[2]

Harvey himself (and I would agree with him) is reluctant to
lay down rigid laws and criteria in advance. At most, one can
indicate the general structure and shape of historical argument.
Basically, the historian is trying to draw conclusions from data.
The data consists most often of written records of some kind,
but it may also include physical artifacts such as buildings,
ruins, monuments, utensils, weapons, and clothing. Under this
heading we could even include an item like George Washington's false teeth, for they provide data for ascertaining information about George Washington himself and about the state of
dental arts in his day. The historian cannot, however, move
directly from the data to the conclusions. He has to satisfy
himself that the data is reliable and that he is interpreting it
responsibly and correctly. He has therefore to examine the
warrants and backing that support the data and also to
anticipate possible objections and special circumstances that
might invalidate his conclusions.

Van Austin Harvey sets out the shape of a historical
argument of this kind in the following diagram.[3]

key

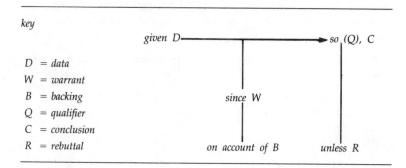

D = *data*
W = *warrant*
B = *backing*
Q = *qualifier*
C = *conclusion*
R = *rebuttal*

As an example of how it works, Harvey takes the claim that Jesus was crucified by the Romans because he was judged to have been a political enemy. The basic data (D) is the commonly agreed fact that Jesus was crucified by the Romans. The conclusion is supported by the warrant (W) that the Romans generally reserved crucifixion for political prisoners. This warrant is supported by well-attested backing (B) which consists of historical reports from a variety of other sources. Hence, the likely (Q) conclusion (C) may be drawn that Jesus was judged by the Romans to have been a political enemy. However, this conclusion may be rebutted (R) if it can be shown that an exception was made in this particular case because of special circumstances. Such circumstances might include a desire on the part of the Romans to please the Jewish authorities.[4]

In historical judgments there are so many kinds of arguments, considerations, and disciplines involved that Harvey prefers to speak of history as a "field-encompassing field."[5] Here, as in other disciplines (including law, medicine, and the natural sciences), much depends on the skill and discernment of the investigator. There are certain procedures in looking at evidence, and certain types of questions that the historian puts to himself and to others when he evaluates their work. I myself would say that in general these are to be defended and justified in retrospect rather than established a priori. Whether any particular procedure applies to a particular question depends on the question and the data available. Some questions can now be dealt with through use of computer science. But these are questions that can be decided only if the appropriate data are available and amenable to statistical analysis.[6] Some questions can be answered in this way, but others cannot.

Sir Lewis Namier, the great authority on eighteenth-century

English history and politics, drew attention to the role of sensitivity in relation to sound historical method when he observed:

> A dilettante is one who takes himself more seriously than his work; and doctrinaires enamoured of their theories or ingenious ideas are dilettanti in public affairs. On the contrary, the historical approach is intellectually humble; the aim is to comprehend situations, to study trends, to discover how things work: and the crowning attainment of historical study is a historical sense—an intuitive understanding of how things do not happen (how they did happen is a matter of specific history).[7]

Harvey speaks of establishing certain presumptions in a field, and it is in the light of these presumptions that subsequent workers in the field frame and answer their questions.

> By virtue of their exhaustive work, certain presumptions have been established, and these presumptions cast something like the "burden of proof" of legal argument on those who would establish a different thesis. This burden alters the dynamics of argument in subtle ways, conveying a certain weight to this or that argument and lending special importance to this or that rebuttal. The skill of the historian is manifested in his degree of sensitivity to these dynamics. He must know what the crucial questions are, where the weak links in other interpretations lie, which data need to be challenged, and which have been misinterpreted.[8]

Harvey does not mean that history is an entirely subjective affair. He goes on to say, "Although there is this almost intangible element in historical judgment, it does not follow that these judgments cannot be justified, or that it is meaningless to ask for evidence and warrants in each case."[9] We must recognize, however, that there are different types of historical judgments and correspondingly varying degrees of verifiability.

Facts, Causes, and Hypotheses

In passing judgments on historical questions we have to recognize that some judgments are more certain and demonstrable than others. The late American archaeologist W. F. Albright gave recognition to this fact when he drew up the following table of historical judgments. The table operates with a descending scale of verifiability. Class 1 contains those judgments that are most easily verifiable. Class 5 contains those that are least open to objective testing and that involve an element of subjective interpretation.

1. Judgments of (about) Typical Occurrence
   The logical basis is inductive and statistical.
2. Judgments of (about) Particular Facts
   Based on public observation and report, subject to repeated testing, or on verifiable evidence of scientific nature—e.g., astronomically fixed dates, medically established cause of death, etc.
3. Judgments of (about) Cause and Effect
4. Judgments of (about) Value
   Subjective ancient or modern, personal or public opinion.
5. Judgments of (about) Personal Reactions.[10]

Some might object that such a tabulation is too rigid or that there are other possibilities and categories or that the final two categories are too vague to admit objective judgment. Nevertheless, the table is useful as long as we keep in mind that within these categories there is room for degrees of certainty, even in judgments concerning typical occurrence. Inferences from statistics may vary wildly—as can be seen all too clearly in the realm of economics, to the embarrassment of politicians and economists alike. On the other hand, it is normally easier to establish what happened and why in the case of a single, well-documented, recent event than in that of something remote and complex. Thus we can say why Edward Heath resigned as British prime minister in 1974: it was because his party lost the general election, and under the British parliamentary system defeated prime ministers tender their resignations to the sovereign who invites the leader of the majority party to form a government. It is a much more difficult business to say why the Roman Empire declined and finally fell or to specify and assess the relative strengths of the causes of the First World War. Nevertheless, there must have been causes, however complex and heterogeneous, for there are no causeless events. If history is to rise above mere antiquarianism, fascinated by the quaintness of isolated objects, such attempts have to be made.[11]

We may repeat what has already been said: historical facts are not items of information to which the historian has direct access but are inferences drawn often from a widely diverse range of information.[12] Similarly, the explanations of the historian are not propositional statements about directly observable events but are hypotheses put forward to account for data at hand. As such, they may be tested by seeing whether they fit the data of the case in question and whether at the same time they agree with other accepted knowledge. The historian may be compared to a detective testing theories against evidence or to a shoe salesperson trying pairs of shoes on people's feet. The process is neither purely inductive nor purely deductive.[13] The historian needs imagination and sense in the framing of his theories (as does the salesperson in selecting suitable shoes). He then tests *the theory* against the data he is evaluating. It is possible for the theory (like the shoes) to be too tight or too slack. In the former case the data (like our toes) are pinched. Something has to be manipulated or even left out. In the latter case the explanation takes account of the data but is not precise enough. It lacks the elegance which is a goal not only of fashion but also of scientific theory. It is the duty of the historian to go on trying new or modified theories until he is satisfied that the theory fits all the data before him in a way that is consonant with his wider view of reality and which is appropriate to the subject matter involved.[14] (Or, if we are to keep the picture of the shoe salesperson, shoes must be found that not only fit the feet of the customer but also suit the customer's particular requirements).[15]

It may be that no such theory can be produced. In that case he has to suspend judgment as a historian though he may still entertain his beliefs and views, acknowledging them for what they are. Perhaps no single explanation can be established to the exclusion of others. In such cases the historian has to keep before himself the various possibilities and probabilities. Here the believer is no exception. Although he may be convinced of the fundamental truth of his beliefs, there may be many aspects of the latter where he has to suspend academic judgment, admitting that he is not in a position to demonstrate the point and granting the possibility of alternative explanations.[16]

The same procedure applies when the historian has to answer questions like "What was the cause of this event?" "Who was really responsible for that situation?" "Was so-and-so a great statesman or just a scheming politician?" In some cases the historian's answer may fit the data so well as to be beyond all reasonable doubt. In other cases the answer may seem to leave out important considerations. Alternatively, it may be put forward as a tentative account, as the best explanation the historian can offer in the absence of firmer evidence. The reputation of the historian as a knowledgeable scholar who is known to have made good judgments in the past certainly has some bearing on the credibility of his ideas. However, in the end the historian comes before the public not as someone whose reputation alone suffices to guarantee the truth of what he says but as someone whose work is open to public scrutiny. It is open to assessment by anyone who is capable of understanding the issues and who has the necessary skills to evaluate the argument. This applies as much in the realm of theological criticism as it does in secular history. By their hypotheses and methods of verification ye shall know them.

We have talked in very general terms about verifiability. How this works out in practice depends on the subject in question. In some fields historical questions of archaeology will play a decisive part. In others it will play no part at all. In some questions of New Testament interpretation the Jewish background will be absolutely crucial to understanding what is going on. In other questions a knowledge of the Graeco-Roman world may be more helpful. But very often the historian will have to draw on a combination of skills and understanding of different backgrounds in order to test ideas.

Because Christianity is so deeply rooted in history, whatever means and techniques are appropriate to the study of history are, in principle, relevant to the study of Christianity. This is not to say that when these means and techniques have been applied to Christianity every problem will be solved. Christianity is more than historical reconstruction. To know its meaning involves repentance, faith, love, and hope. Only in this way can one become, as Kierkegaard would have said, a "contemporary" of Christ. On the other hand, to understand the Christian revelation in its concrete, historical expression, we must study it in the light of the disciplines of textual criticism, linguistics, and literary and historical criticism. Such study involves not only questions of authorship and date of documents but a historical appreciation of their background, form, tendencies, and thought world as they relate to the information that these documents contain.

This is not the place to attempt to survey these issues. [17] On the other hand, I must underline the point that I am *not* endorsing each and every technique favored by whatever happens to be the most vocal school of thought at any given time. The same hard-headed caution has to be applied here as in any other academic discipline. What today might seem to be an impressive road to discovery may tomorrow turn out to be a blind alley. A case in point is the criteria used by Bultmann and his followers for determining the authenticity of Jesus' sayings. As is now widely recognized, these criteria will not stand up to close scrutiny.[18] Here, as anywhere else, the validity of the results depends on the validity of the methods.

The Crucial Question of Analogy

Nowhere is the point more crucial than in the contemporary debate on hermeneutics.[19] Here the central question is that of the interpretation of Jesus and the gospel. The traditional Christian approach, as represented by Reformed theology down to the present day, sees Scripture as the record of God's revelation of himself in the history and writings of the people of Israel and supremely in Jesus Christ. This record was written by men inspired by the Holy Spirit, who guided their insights and writing. The ultimate basis for this view is the testimony of the writers themselves and the teaching of Jesus, acknowledged by the believer not only as historically authoritative but as the Word of God in his own life and experience. The same authority is the basis for taking Scripture as decisive and normative not only for our perspectives and understanding of life but also for the theistic interpretation of history. God acts in history, and supremely so in the life, death, and resurrection of Jesus, which constitute God's decisive revelation of himself to man.

The Bultmann school, on the other hand, refused to admit divine revelations and regarded such accounts as belonging to the primitive perspectives of the prescientific era. The notions of heaven, hell, atonement, and of a divine redeemer are then mythological expressions of man's understanding of his own existence.[20] This is not the place to examine the question of myth in detail.[21] Our concern here is with the fundamental differences of principle and the radically different world views that underlie these conflicting interpretations. Basic to Bultmann's approach are the premises that the world is to be explained in terms of a closed system of natural, historical, and psychological causes that does not admit exceptions or interventions, and that all history must be reinterpreted in the light of contemporary understanding. This view received classical exposition from the pen of Ernst Troeltsch in an essay dating back to 1898, "On Historical and Dogmatic Method in Theology."[22]

Troeltsch believed that history formed a network of interconnecting events. The same kinds of causes and factors that apply today must have been at work in previous ages. How do we decide what to make of a historical report? Do we believe everything we read? How do we distinguish the true from the false? How do we understand events and people? For Troeltsch the key to these questions lay in the principle of analogy.

For the means by which criticism first becomes possible at all is the application of analogy. Analogy with what happens before our eyes and comes to pass in us is the key to criticism. Deception, dubious dealings, fabrication of myth, fraud and party spirit which we see before our eyes are the means by which we recognize the same kind of thing in the material which comes to us. Agreement with normal, ordinary, repeatedly attested modes of occurrence and conditions, as we know them, is the mark of probability for the occurrences which criticism can acknowledge as having really happened or leave aside. The observation of analogies between homogeneous occurrences of the past makes it possible to ascribe probability to them and to interpret what is unknown in the one by the known in the other. The universal power of analogy includes the essential homogeneity [German: *Gleichartigkeit*] of all historical events. Admittedly this is not an identity [German: *Gleichheit*]; it leaves all possible room for differences. However, on each occasion it presupposes a nucleus of common homogeneity, from which the differences can be understood and felt.[23]

Clearly, Troeltsch is saying something important here. Comparison of the new and unknown with the known plays an important part in human knowledge. If we have not the remotest experience of a thing, it is impossible to conceive what that thing is like. I do not think that the historian can or should try to avoid interpreting new data in the light of his present understanding, but it seems wrong to say that the historian must have had precisely the same passions and ambitions as Genghis Kahn or Adolf Hitler or even as Lloyd George or Franklin D. Roosevelt in order to understand these men. Still less does he need to have suffered personally at their hands. Indeed, too close a personal involvement can also distort. But the historian does need sympathetic imagination to try to put him- or herself in their place and in the place of those with whom they came into contact. We must also ask another question, however: Does not the rigid application of the doctrine of analogy actually preclude the apprehension of the unique—even before we have looked at it?

Wolfhart Pannenberg is nearer the mark when he redefines the use of analogy as follows:

The cognitive power of analogy depends upon the fact that it teaches us to see contents of the same kind in *nonhomogeneous things [das Gleichartige im Ungleichartigen]*. If the historian keeps his eye on the nonexchangeable individuality and contingency of an event, then he will see that he is dealing with nonhomogeneous things, which cannot be contained without remainder in any analogy.[24]

This is not to say that we must weave our net with holes so wide that they let in each and every myth and legend. To quote Pannenberg again:

> That a reported event bursts analogies with otherwise usual or repeatedly attested events is still no ground for disputing its facticity. It is another matter when positive analogies to forms of tradition (such as myths and even legends) relating to unreal objects, phenomena referring to states of consciousness (like visions) may be found in the historical sources. In such cases historical understanding guided by analogy can lead to a negative judgment about the reality of the occurrences reported in the tradition. Such a judgment will be rendered not because of the unusualness of something reported about, but rather because it exhibits a positive analogy to some form of consciousness which has no objective referent.[25]

Miracles are examples of alleged events that burst analogy with our normal, everyday experience. They confront us with the question "Should we reject all miracle stories outright if we have never experienced a miracle for ourselves?" Or, if we accept, say, miracle stories in the Bible but not those handed down from the medieval church, we have to face the question "Why believe some but not others?" But the prime example of an event bursting all analogy with our ordinary experience is the resurrection of Jesus.

In all these questions the issue turns on analogy. If I allow my own limited experience to be the measure of all things, I will surely cut reality down to my size. If, however, I see reasons why an event might be feasible, and I have attestation for that event, the dynamics of the argument will be changed. I then become able to recognize objective reality in the event even though I may not be able to understand it. We need to look for analogies between our present understanding of history and the data we are examining. But we must be careful not to overpress them and reject out of hand what does not seem to fit.

This applies both on a secular level and when we are dealing with the allegedly supernatural. Moreover, analogy works two ways. We use analogies with the present in order to understand the past, but we also use analogies with the past in order to understand the present. Here too there are many traps for the unwary. Sir Lewis Namier has some timely warnings on the need for caution. In answer to the question "Can men learn from history?" he replies:

That depends on the quality and accuracy of the historian's perceptions and conclusions, and on the critical faculties of the reader—in the "argument," and on the "intellects" to comprehend it. When erudition exceeds intelligence, past results are rigidly applied to radically changed situations and preparations are completed for fighting the previous war. . . . The price paid . . . in the trench-warfare of 1914–18 produced in turn the Maginot mentality among the French public and politicians. . . . The time lag in disciplined military thought is aggravated on the victorious side by the glory which attaches to past success and by the prestige of their aging artificers. Yet in all spheres alike, even in the freest, false analogies, the product of superficial knowledge and reasoning, are the pitfall of history as *magistra vitae*.[26]

Here, of course, Namier is talking about secular history in secular terms. But the same applies to religious history.

To my mind two points stand out in all this. (1) We need to be extremely sensitive and careful in seeing and applying analogies; and (2) our present understanding needs to be perpetually revised and enlarged in the light of new knowledge. The latter must be allowed to include new knowledge of the past. Unless our understanding is broadly based and open-ended, progress in knowledge is impossible.

In reading biblical history, the ordinary Christian, no less than the critical historian, repeatedly makes use of analogy whether he or she is conscious of doing so or not. When a person identifies oneself with this or that character or sees a contemporary situation paralleled by something in Scripture or draws some lesson, that person is implicitly employing the principle of analogy. But in believing, say, in the resurrection of Jesus, even though one has no experience of the dead being raised, he or she is doing what Pannenberg recommends. The person is affirming belief in the unique which bursts analogies with present experience. In the last analysis the issue between the traditional understanding of Christianity and that of Bultmann and the radicals comes down to the question of analogy. The Bultmann school insists that the witness of the New Testament must be understood in the light of the closed scientific world view that it holds, and hence must be "demythologized." Traditional Protestant and Catholic theologians reply that this rigid use of analogy has prevented Bultmann from recognizing the unique.

Professor T. F. Torrance goes even further, accusing the Bultmann school of a lack of objectivity. In any science the object studied must determine the methods employed. In the case of Christian theology we are concerned with the revelation of God. It is this revelation in all its concreteness that must determine our methods and modify our presuppositions.[27] For the Bultmann school the problem is: How do we think of Jesus Christ in the light of our scientific world view and closed view of history, which do not admit supernatural interventions? Torrance inverts the question. How do we think of space and time, *given* the Incarnation and modern physics? He holds that the former view, which preconceives and thus misconceives the question, may be traced back to Greek philosophy, which influenced the medieval West and thence Lutheranism, which in turn set the pace for modern theology. Bultmann's way of posing the problem is preeminently an heir to this tradition, which views space and time as a receptacle in which things exist and happen, thus predetermining their shape and possibility. Torrance traces his own view back through Reformed theology to the Nicene fathers, Athanasius, and Origen. In connection with the latter he declares:

> The incarnation means that He by whom all things are comprehended and contained by assuming a body made room for Himself in our physical existence, yet without being contained, confined or circumscribed in place as in a vessel. He was wholly present in the body and yet wholly present everywhere, for He became man without ceasing to be God![28]

Space is a *differential* concept that is essentially *open-ended*, "for it is defined in accordance with the interaction between God and man, eternal and contingent happening."[29] In an objective and disciplined theology

> the scientific function of theological statements is to offer a rational account of knowledge beyond the limits of mere this-worldly experience through the use of acknowledged concepts taken from this world, and so to help our minds to lay hold upon it even though it is more than we can grasp within the limits of these concepts. Theological statements properly made are thus by way of being operational statements directing us toward what is new and beyond but which cannot be wholly indicated or explained in terms of the old . . . . theological statements operate . . . with essentially *open concepts*— concepts that are relatively closed on our side of their reference through their connection with the space-time structures of our world, but which on God's side are wide open to the infinite objectivity and inexhaustible intelligibility of the divine Being.[30]

There is a sense in which Judaism and the biblical writers have a concept of analogy. But in one way, at least, it seems to invert that of Troeltsch. Whereas Troeltsch measures the past in the light of his understanding of the present, the biblical writers measure the present in the light of their understanding of the past.[31] The psalmist strengthens faith and builds up hope by calling to mind the great deeds of God.[32] Peter seeks to put the plight of his readers in perspective by addressing them as "exiles of the Dispersion," "a chosen race, a royal priesthood, a holy nation, God's own people," and as "aliens and exiles."[33] The history and the imagery of the past is applied to the present in order to reveal dimensions of the situation that would otherwise be concealed.

A particular case of this is the notion of fulfillment, which in the hands of the New Testament writers is not simply a case of noting predictions that have come about.[34] Indeed, if we treat some of their examples as such instances, we may conclude that they look rather forced and trivial. The context of Hosea 11:1 ("Out of Egypt I called my son") does not suggest that the prophet foresaw the holy family returning as refugees from Egypt (cf. Matt. 2:15). And similarly, the context of Jeremiah 31:15 does not suggest that the prophet predicted the slaughter of the innocents at Bethlehem that took place so many hundreds of years after his death (cf. Matt. 2:18). But the passages in question demand a more profound interpretation. Matthew is saying, in effect, that these new events that fulfill prophecy are to be understood in the perspective of the original event. In a sense they reduplicate the latter. Whereas the believing Jew regarded the Exodus as a great landmark in history, this apparently insignificant event of a single family returning from Egypt is just as much the work of God. In fact, it is even more significant.

In biblical history the concept of God is continually being enlarged and modified. The biblical writers tell us that if we wish to know God and understand what he is doing, we must reflect on his dealings with Israel. There is a kind of continuous, reciprocal interpretation of the past by the present and of the present by the past. This operates within biblical history itself. The history of Jesus completes and modifies earlier understanding. Pannenberg comments:

> This concept of God will become a proper concept of a theology based on revelation only . . . by the correction and transformation it undergoes in its application to the God of Israel: that is, by its referral to the history in which the character of this God first disclosed itself step by step, then finally and with ultimate validity in the presence of the eschaton in the fate of Jesus of Nazareth. True knowledge of God is obtained from this history for the first time, and therefore cannot be presupposed as something that makes it

possible to grasp this knowledge. It is this history which first corrects the preliminary (and distorted) representations of God—indeed, even Israel's representations of its God! Thus, all statements about the redemptive event remain bound to analogies "from below," whose applicability is subject to the procedures of historical criticism.[35]

The use of analogy works both ways in understanding biblical history, as it does in understanding secular history. We understand the past in the light of the present, but we also understand the present in the light of the past. Understanding grows by a process of successive approximation. To comprehend history we need to make use of whatever techniques are appropriate for the historian; but history itself and the reality it contains must determine our techniques and modify our presuppositions.

3

What Does the Historian Achieve?

Anyone who has ever watched the evening news on television has been watching history. What is shown in the newscasts qualifies as history on two counts. On the one hand, the pictures that we see now belong to the past. On the other hand, they are presented as an accurate record of the past. But just how accurate are they? The leading anchorman on a major American network used to end the newscast each night by saying, "And that's the way it is." But was it really?

To ask this question is not to impugn in any way the sincerity and veracity of the program. It is not to question the hard work and integrity of hundreds, if not thousands, of people whose efforts went into producing the newscasts. But it does not take much reflection to see that a half-hour or even an hour-long newscast cannot represent everything that went on in the world on any given day. Where there were no television cameras, there could be no pictures. Where there were no reporters, there could be no "news." A newscast in Los Angeles will be quite different from one in London, Paris, or Tokyo. Events of world importance may be reported on each of the newscasts but will be angled differently according to the interests of the particular viewing public, and the same event may not get the same priority in each place. Events of national or local interest may not figure at all outside the country concerned.

Of all the media, television is the most illusory—precisely because it gives the appearance of being the most objective. After all, are we not seeing pictures of events before our very eyes? Surely there can be nothing more objective than that! But again, a moment's reflection will tell us that the cameras had to be put there. Someone had to make a decision about what to film and what not to film. Moreover, for every few feet of film shown, there must be hundreds of feet discarded. The editorial department decides not only what are the best pictures but what are the best pictures worth showing. On top of that there is always a reporter or studio anchorperson to tell us what we are watching and what the significance of it all is.

Television reporting is not a window on the world through which we see whatever happens to pass by. It is a highly selective process that represents only the minutest fraction of all events that have happened. It cannot represent anything without also interpreting it, for representation without interpretation is an impossibility. To say all this is in no way to denigrate the media. It is simply to recognize some of the factors involved in reporting the past, however recent or remote.

Objectivity?

The same applies to all attempts to write history. Early in the nineteenth century the great German historian Leopold von Ranke declared that his aim in writing history was simply to show *"wie es eigentlich gewesen"*—"how it actually was." The remark is one of the most celebrated pronouncements ever made by a historian. But since Ranke's day the statement has frequently been held up to ridicule. To be fair to Ranke, the sentence should be quoted in full: "People have assigned to history the office of judging the past and instructing the present generation for the benefit of future ages: the present attempt does not aspire to such high offices: it merely wants to show how it actually was."[1] In context this is not a statement of presumption but of modesty. It is a declaration that the primary goal of the historian is to get at the truth as it happened.

However, historians who are usually labeled relativists have seriously questioned whether Ranke's goal is realistic. This questioning has taken two main lines. On the one hand, it is urged that it is naïve to suppose that history is a matter of presenting "all the facts" and then letting them "speak for themselves."[2] Indeed, history involves making value judgments. On the other hand, we are reminded that the historian never has access to all the facts. And from those that he has, he has to select. History, it is therefore said, is relative to the historian who himself reflects a particular culture and particular interests and standpoints.

Value Judgments

The thesis that history involves value judgments has been argued convincingly by Sir Isaiah Berlin in his lecture *Historical Inevitability*. History involves moral judgments because it is dealing with human beings, and as such it should not be confused with the natural sciences.

> The invocation to historians to suppress even that minimal degree of moral or psychological evaluation which is necessarily involved in viewing human beings as creatures with purposes and motives (and not merely as causal factors in the procession of events), seems to me to rest upon a confusion of the aims and methods of the humane studies with those of natural science. It is one of the greatest and most destructive fallacies of the last hundred years.[3]

On the other hand, Sir Herbert Butterfield has argued that "moral judgments on human beings are by their nature irrelevant to the enquiry and alien to the intellectual realm of scientific history." For the latter is concerned with "just the observable interconnections of events."[4] William H. Dray argues that, in so far as history is concerned with the study of human actions and therefore may be expressed in *purposive* terms, moral evaluation is not necessary.[5]

In response to Butterfield and Dray, I want to say that human interconnections cannot be described without invoking moral terms, however covertly. As Dray himself concedes, to describe an act as "murder" involves a moral value judgment. From a purely physical point of view, the same act could be described as a "killing." But as a matter of practice, historians do not go through their writings crossing out the word "murder" in those cases which they think require it. In so doing, they are making an implicit moral judgment, implying moral responsibility. Moreover, to suspend a moral judgment is just as much a moral act as to make a positive moral judgment. The same applies to the whole range of words covering human activities. Some, of course, are neutral in that they do not involve moral judgments. But to use a neutral word instead of one expressing some kind of evaluation may itself involve making a moral judgment.

The decision whether to use the word "murder" or the word "killing" depends partly though not entirely on one's perspective. Some moral judgments (like psychological judgments) will depend on the standpoint of the observer. In this sense they are relative to his judgment and criteria. They may be subjective in that they represent a purely personal attitude, but they may be

objective in so far as they represent values that are independent
of the individual thinker. Ranke's reaction to didactic history
(which is more interested in drawing morals and using the past
for propaganda purposes) was a healthy one. But if the above
argument is valid, neither the past nor the present can be rid of
values. We cannot expunge moral issues from the past, nor can
we avoid making moral judgments in trying to discern what the
moral issues were. What we have said about moral judgment
applies as well to the assessment of other factors, such as
psychological, economic, sociological, and religious causes. Our
assessment of these factors will be relative to our standpoint.
This is not to say that they will necessarily be arbitrary. That
will depend on the overall validity of our standpoint, on its
relevance to the subject we are considering, and on the use we
make of it. But it does mean that the account we give will
represent a perspective or a combination of perspectives.

Selection and Perspectives

There is an element of selection in the choice of our
standpoints. There is also an element of selection (both
voluntary and involuntary) in the historian's handling of his
material. One of the most important statements of the relativist
case is a paper by the American historian Charles A. Beard
entitled "That Noble Dream" (1935).[6] Beard argues, for example, that

> the historian is not an observer of the past that lies beyond his own
> time. He cannot see it *objectively* as the chemist sees his test tubes
> and compounds. The historian must "see" the actuality of history
> through the medium of documentation. That is his sole recourse.[7]

But many events and personalities "escape the recording of
documentation," and "in very few cases can the historian be
reasonably sure that he has assembled all the documents of a
given period, region, or segment."[8] Thus the "total actuality is
not factually knowable to an historian." The historian is never
"a neutral mirror." "Whatever acts of purification the historian
may perform he yet remains human, a creature of time, place,
circumstance, interests, predilections, culture."[9] "He may
search for, but he cannot find, the 'objective truth' of history, or
write it, 'as it actually was.' "[10]
We cannot but agree with Beard that history involves
selection. It is a selection that is partly done for him by the
preservation (conscious and unconscious) of material. But out
of this material the historian will select what is significant to

him in the light of the questions he is asking. It is this process that led Jakob Burckhardt to describe history as "the record of facts which one age finds remarkable in another."[11] But whether a fact is remarkable depends on why it is remarkable. When seen within one framework of thought a fact may not be particularly significant, but when it is seen within another it may take on quite a different meaning.[12] To the Roman historian Tacitus, Christ was a man who "suffered the extreme penalty during the reign of Tiberius at the hands of one of our procurators, Pontius Pilate."[13] He is noted only because his followers happened to suffer abominable torments at the hands of Nero who is the immediate object of Tacitus's interest. To the Evangelists and other New Testament writers Christ's death has a quite different significance. It is not that there is any substantial difference of opinion as to what happened, though the Evangelists supply much more detail. It is the framework or perspective that is decisive here.

History books differ not only because some historians are more diligent and perceptive than others but also because they write from different perspectives. It is not necessarily a case of one perspective being right and another wrong. Just as geographical textbooks contain some maps that give the physical features of a region and others that give political ones, and some a combination of both, so historical subjects are capable of being studied from different and complementary standpoints. Moreover, just as there are different kinds of map projections and conventions made necessary by the attempt to reduce multidimensional reality to two dimensions, so inevitably the attempt to reduce people and events to verbal narrative means the employment of conventions, projections, and imaginative interpretation.[14]

No single account can show exhaustively the course of history as it happened, for no single account can look at everything from all points of view. The most that the historian can do is to look at his or her subject in relation to certain questions. The historian then has to leave it to others (or come back to the subject) to bring out other aspects of the subject. By putting different accounts together, we may be able to obtain a better understanding of events, personalities, and issues than we could if we just looked at them from one vantage point. But it is humanly impossible to see everything all at once. Moreover, we have to reckon with the fact that resources may be limited. And for that reason our accounts may be limited. To say this is far from saying that no knowledge of the past is possible. But it leads us back once more to the question of what the historian really does achieve.

Reconstruction?

When people talk about history they often talk about reconstructing the past. I myself have come to think that this is not the best way of talking about it. History is not reconstruction in the normal sense of the word. It is not like reconstructing vintage automobiles, airplanes, trams, railway locomotives, or old houses. In such cases there may be certain pieces of the original thing to work on. By use of original plans, research, and hard work, people can make something *like* the original in as much detail as possible and *on the same scale*. But the events and personalities of the past cannot be reconstructed in this way. We cannot bring the dead back to life for an action replay. We may get fragments from the past (artifacts, records, clothes, etc.), but we cannot go back into the past. Moreover, we may not possess sufficient continuous records to be able to make a full-scale reconstruction. The nearest we get to this is the historical tableau and television documentary in which actors speak the lines originally spoken. But if such a tableau consists merely in repeating recorded lines and actions, it lacks the interpretative element which is an essential feature of critical history. And if the tableau is so arranged as to bring out this or that emphasis, an element of selection and interpretation is clearly involved so that it ceases to be a mere reconstruction.

However, most history writing does not take such a form. Most of it takes the form of written historical judgments based on evaluation of data and opinions.[15] What then is involved? Sir Lewis Namier has put forward the thesis that

> as history deals with concrete events fixed in time and space, narrative is its basic medium—but guided by analytic selection of what to narrate. The function of the historian is akin to that of the painter and not of the photographic camera: to discover and set forth, to single out and stress that which is of the nature of the thing, and not to reproduce indiscriminately all that meets the eye. To distinguish a tree you look at its shape, its bark and leaf; counting and measuring the branches would get you nowhere. Similarly what matters in history is the great outline and the significant detail; what must be avoided is the deadly mass of irrelevant narrative.[16]

This, of course, is not an open invitation to take shortcuts and to make impressionistic caricatures instead of doing painstaking investigation. Accuracy, as A. E. Housman remarked, "is a duty, not a virtue."[17] Indeed, Namier's own work was characterized by tremendous industry and attention to detail. Rather, Namier is saying that the aim the historian should keep before him is to discern what is significant, and he sees this as "the great outline and the significant detail."

It may be remarked how closely the biblical writers come in their own particular ways to the notion of history as "the great outline and the significant detail." Admittedly, they did not set out to produce pieces of critical history in the modern sense, but to demand this of any ancient writer is to set up an arbitrary criterion. Any ancient—or any modern—writing must be understood in terms of what it is trying to do and in the light of its particular conventions. These writings had their conventions and operated on the basis of what we have called their "projections." Different conventions and projections are to be found in different parts of the Bible. They are not all written on the same scale. The reporting by Matthew, Mark, and Luke of the sayings and actions of Jesus is different from that of the early chapters of Genesis, which report cosmic events in terms of words and actions. The standpoint of the fourth Gospel is different from that of the first three Gospels, and the standpoint of each of the latter is markedly different from that of the others. To say this is not to agree with the nineteenth-century critics that one of them is right and that the others are later elaborations. Rather, it is to say that each must be understood on its own terms before anything further can be said. The biblical writers do not ask psychological and economic questions. They see events and people in terms of righteousness and the will of God. Consequently, the New Testament writers see events and people within the framework of law, prophecy, apocalyptic imagery, and messianic expectation.

We should not expect ancient writers to observe the same distinctions between direct speech and indirect speech as we would today. There are no quotation marks in the ancient languages and, in my opinion, it is misleading when modern translations insert them. For they give the impression of verbatim precision in recorded speech, an intention not present in the original.[18] What is given by the Evangelists is not a series of verbatim quotations but a report of the main thrust of a speaker's utterance, as seen in relation to the event being described. When we look at the Gospels we do not find a balanced biography in the modern sense. Rather, each Evangelist gives, from his own standpoint, a general outline and significant detail. What determines the composition of that outline and detail is the writer's perception of his subject, the resources with which he has to work, and his aims in writing.[19]

Models

Namier compares the work of the historian with that of the painter. So far as it goes, the image is helpful. But, like all illustrations, it has its limitations. The painter is normally able to look at his or her subject, or at least at sketches the artist has previously made. But the historian—unless she or he happened to be there as an eyewitness—does not normally have direct access to the subject. Moreover, the account given by the historian is not a visual representation. Historical accounts consist largely of words, and words are not verbal snapshots of reality.

In describing a person, a place, or an event, the historian is not producing a kind of verbal videotape of who was there and what went on. The historian was not there to see, and in any case does not possess a verbal video camera to catch the scene. Let us for a moment consider a statement such as Mark 1:21: "And they went into Capernaum; and immediately on the sabbath he [Jesus] entered the synagogue and taught" (RSV). Mark is not trying to transfer the picture that he has in his mind to our minds, for we cannot see what he or his sources saw. We do not know what the synagogue actually looked like—or, for that matter, what Jesus looked like. We do not know how many people were in the synagogue at the time. We do not know what time of day it was—or, for that matter, when it was. We do not know what Jesus taught. We are simply told that he taught.

Words do not function like snapshots. They are more like computer codes that activate our memory banks. We have some idea of the meanings of words like "Capernaum," "they," "he," "sabbath," "synagogue," and "taught." When put together in a sentence they activate the memory banks in our minds, and we are able to form some idea of what they refer to. But this idea is not a photograph of the past, nor is it strictly a picture. It may perhaps be compared with a model.

In speaking of models we must frankly acknowledge the limitations of the imagery. Nevertheless, the concept of the model has proved its worth in the philosophy of science, in helping to envisage what scientists are doing in constructing theories about the physical world.[20] In a similar way the activity of the historian may be compared with that of the model maker.

Like scientific theory, historical construction is not a literal description of what is observed. As we have already seen, it is not exactly a reconstruction of reality. It is more like a model or a series of models. The historian may have incorporated things from the past, such as fragments of utterances, observations, and records. But he will have had to use his own skill, insight, and ingenuity in its construction. What he has made will not be identical with the original thing. It will have its particular scale and conventions. Some things will be represented and not others, depending partly on the material available and partly on the purpose of the model. But if it is well done it will enable the onlooker to have some idea of what the original was like and what significance it has. It will enable him to perceive that original not directly but indirectly.

In history writing this model-making process is a continual one. The initial accounts, say of the life of Jesus in the Gospels, provide one set of models. The accounts of critical historians provide another. The reader's understanding presents yet another set. The process of understanding involves an interaction between the models and the historian (whether a professional critical historian or just an ordinary person thinking about history). It is not that the latest critical reconstruction necessarily supersedes all earlier models or that the primary accounts can ever be dispensed with. But neither can we avoid making our reconstructions, whether they be technical and critical or unreflective. What critical reconstruction does is to attempt to correct unreflective understanding and to see earlier accounts in new perspective and depth. It proceeds by what we earlier called "successive approximation" as it seeks to discern the intelligible structure of the event with which it deals.

The goal of the study of history is not this model-making as an end in itself but rather the apprehension and understanding of reality through it.[21] It was this that led R. G. Collingwood to see history as "the re-enactment of past experience."[22] In so far as God is involved in an event in the past, reflection on that event is the means not only of consciously apprehending God but of apprehending God in a way that reaches beyond the limits of our immediate experience. Many years ago Wilhelm Dilthey observed how understanding opens up possibilities that are just not present within the restrictions of one's normal life.

> The possibility of experiencing religious states in my own existence is narrowly restricted for me as it is for most people today. But when I run through the letters and writings of Luther, the reports of his contemporaries, the records of the religious confrontations and

councils, and his activity as a minister, I experience a religious process of such eruptive force, such energy, in which it is a matter of life and death, that it lies beyond all possibility of actually being lived by a man of our time. But I can relive it. I transpose myself into the circumstances: everything in them drives towards such an extraordinary development of the religious temperament. . . . Unknown objects of beauty in the world and regions of life, which could never be reached personally by a man in his limited circumstances, are opened up before him. To put it in general terms: man, bound and determined by the reality of life, is set free not only by art—as has often been argued—but also by the understanding of history. And this effect of history, which its most modern detractors have not seen, is broadened and deepened in the further stages of historical consciousness.[23]

What Dilthey says here of Luther may be applied to other historical personalities, whether they are connected with Christianity or with any other religion. In this sense Christianity is on the same footing as other religions. But to make this point is simply to recognize that all religions have histories. The decisive difference between them—as between different historical figures—is what they embody in history. Whether new experiences, insights, and horizons are opened up for us depends on two factors: on the one hand, the persons or the events and what they embody, and on the other, our understanding of them. The medium by which this is mediated is history and in particular our historical models.

4

How Does History Affect Belief?

In this final chapter I will focus on two issues that are closely intertwined. The first is the question of the relationship between history and revelation. The second is the importance of history for faith.

History and Revelation

When we talk about revelation we are talking about the way in which God makes himself known to human beings. There is no subject in theology more keenly debated than this. Throughout the ages Christians have testified to their belief that God has spoken through the Scripture of the Old and New Testaments and that these Scriptures are a true record of God's actions in history. But as we saw in chapter 1, it is precisely this claim that God has spoken and acted in history that lies at the center of the battle that has been going on since the Age of Enlightenment.[1]

If the accounts that the Bible gives are inaccurate and unhistorical, can the Bible be regarded as God's Word? Can we even speak of revelation if what people believe to be revealed turns out to be at variance with accepted facts? Common sense tells us that the answer to these questions must be "No!" In this at least the skeptic and the believer are in agreement. What divides them is the question of the validity of the truth claims of the Bible. In the words of the 1978 *Chicago Statement on Biblical Inerrancy*,

> The authority of Scripture is a key issue for the Christian Church in this and every age. Those who profess faith in Jesus Christ as Lord and Savior are called to show the reality of their discipleship by humbly and faithfully obeying God's written Word. To stray from Scripture in faith or conduct is disloyalty to our Master. Recognition

of the total truth and trustworthiness of Holy Scripture is essential to a full grasp and adequate confession of its authority.[2]

Underlying these challenging words is the conviction that "the written Word in its entirety is revelation given by God."[3] To say this is not necessarily to deny that God discloses himself through other means such as in nature. On the other hand, the statement clearly treats God's self-disclosure in and through Scripture as fundamental to Christian faith and practice.[4]

The dispute over revelation is not simply an argument between believers and unbelievers. Within the Christian church there is an ongoing debate about the nature of revelation in the light of the attempt to understand the Bible as history.[5] Broadly speaking, there are two opposing camps: those who see revelation as revelation of the Word of God and those who see revelation as history. To leave it at that, however, would be to oversimplify, for the theologians of the Word range from the Reformers to Bultmann. And the protagonists of revelation in history include those who see it as Israelite history and those who see it as universal history. Some contemporary scholars would like to scrap the idea of revelation altogether. But there are others, including myself, who believe that a Christian view of revelation must embrace revelation in history (both biblical and universal history), revelation through the Word of God, and revelation in on-going human experience.

Between 1945 and 1960 there flourished what came to be known as the Biblical Theology Movement. This movement fell far short of embracing the positions stated in the Chicago Inerrancy Statement. But it stressed the uniqueness of the Bible and emphasized divine revelation in history. For any who shared this view, biblical theology was the recital of God's acts in history. Thus G. Ernest Wright could say that one of the distinctive characteristics of the Bible was to see history and historical tradition "as the primary sphere in which God reveals himself."[6] Wright went on to say:

> To be sure, God also reveals himself and his will in various ways to the inner consciousness of man, as in other religions. Yet the nature and content of this inner revelation is determined by the outward, objective happenings of history in which individuals are called to participate. It is, therefore, the objectivity of God's historical acts which are the focus of attention, not the subjectivity of inner, emotional, diffuse and mystical experience.[7]

This view of history in the Old Testament found expression in the concept of God's "election of a special people through whom he would accomplish his purposes."[8] Belief in election provided the framework for understanding not only the migration of Abraham to Canaan and the exodus deliverance, but life in Palestine, prophetic eschatology, and the apocalyptic of the Book of Daniel. God's election of Israel was confirmed and clarified on Sinai. Israel's subsequent sin was seen as a breach of the covenant which enabled the faithful to see that election was unalterable. Wright's view represents a fairly conservative approach to Old Testament history. Revelation is mediated through history, the revelation being the significance of events as indicative of the mind and character of God.

But others have denied that revelation has any factual content. In his Gifford Lectures in the 1930s, William Temple put forward a view of revelation that drove a sharp wedge between encounter with God and any empirical content that such an encounter might have. "What is offered to man's apprehension in any specific Revelation is not truth concerning God but the living God Himself."[9] Temple was particularly concerned to get away from the idea of revealed truth. "There is no such thing as revealed truth. There are truths of revelation, that is to say, propositions which express the results of correct thinking concerning revelation; but they are not themselves directly revealed."[10]

Rudolf Bultmann was even more concerned to remove all factual content from revelation. He answered the question "What then has been revealed according to the New Testament?" by saying:

> Nothing at all, so far as the question concerning revelation asks for doctrines—doctrines, say, that no man could have discovered for himself—or for mysteries that become known once and for all as soon as they are communicated. On the other hand, however, *everything has been revealed, insofar as man's eyes are opened concerning his own existence and he is once again able to understand himself. . . .* Revelation is an act of God, an *occurrence*, and not a communication of supernatural knowledge.[11]

The demand to say what the Word of God is must be rejected because it rests on the idea that it is possible to designate a complex of statements that can be found and understood with respect to "content."

Formal clarification of what is meant by the Word of God in Scripture, Bultmann claimed, shows us only that "no 'content' of the Word of God can be exhibited, but rather can only be heard in the immediate moment."[12] Faith, for Bultmann, does not have an object. It "does not relate itself to historical or cosmic processes that could be established as free from doubt but rather to the *preaching* behind which faith cannot go and which says to man that he must understand the cross as God's act of salvation and believe in the resurrection."[13] The context of Bultmann's thought makes it clear that the "cross" and 'resurrection" are not to be understood as empirical, historical events, but as symbols designating the limits of man's existence and thought.[14] Faith is a *venture.* It is a decision to let my concrete existence here and now "be determined by the proclamation and faith in it."[15]

Some have even gone beyond Bultmann. Among them is F. G. Downing. Whereas Bultmann at least retained the idea of revelation, Downing proposes to abandon it altogether.

> If God intended to "reveal himself" in Christ, in the events of his life and death and resurrection and in his teaching, he failed. It seems more faithful to assume that this was not his intention. . . . A "revelation" of what cannot now be seen is not a "revelation." We may believe, trust, that Christ has made the "revealing of God" a possibility in some sort of future. It is surely nonsense, even pernicious nonsense, to pretend that it is a present fact.[16]

Over against Temple, Bultmann, and Downing, with their stress on a factually contentless (and in Downing's case, a nonexistent) revelation, we may turn back to others who see revelation as having some objective content (whether it be in event or word). Oscar Cullmann, for example, insists that faith must have an object:

> The basis for this separation between an objective event on the one hand, and my faith in it and my decision on the other, is not an "unconscious," antiquated philosophy of the separation between object and subject, outdated by existentialism, as the theologians influenced by Heidegger assert. It is the plain and simple New Testament concept of faith as it is developed especially clearly in Paul. *The act of faith itself requires this distinction.* Faith means that in humility I turn away from myself and look only to the radiant light of an event in which I am totally uninvolved, so that I can only fall down in worship before him who has brought about this event (Rom. 1.21). As I humbly turn away from myself and look to the event, I appropriate the event in faith. Faith means excluding myself and thus including myself. *So I gain my self-understanding when I am not observing my self-understanding.* Therein lies the paradox of New Testament faith.[17]

Few theologians have more vigorously defended the otherness of God than Karl Barth. With William Temple he could insist that "what God speaks is never known or true anywhere in abstraction from God Himself. It is known and true in and through the fact that He Himself says it, that He is present in person in and with what is said by Him."[18] Barth's view of revelation is personal and dynamic. But just as we do not know people fully apart from what they say,[19] so we do not know God by purely mystical illumination. Knowing a person is not like watching a mime and guessing at what he or she is trying to communicate. Nor is it like watching a television program with the sound turned off. Words are not everything, but without them we are not fully personal. Communication involves more than words, but without them communication is virtually impossible. For this reason Barth could go on to say that

> God does reveal Himself in statements, through the medium of speech, and indeed of human speech. His word is always this or that word spoken by the prophets and apostles and proclaimed in the Church. The personal character of God's Word is not, then, to be played off against its verbal or spiritual character.[20]

In speaking of the Word of God, Barth maintained that God's Word has a threefold form. As the revelation of the Father, Jesus Christ is the revealed Word of God in the strictest sense of the term.[21] But Scripture is also the Word of God in written form. In addition to these two forms of the Word of God, there is also the proclaimed Word of God in Christian witness and testimony. Insofar as God speaks to people through this testimony, Barth believed that we are entitled to think of it as a form of the Word of God. But such a testimony is not a new revelation. Indeed, Barth believed that all three forms of the Word of God are interrelated.

> The revealed Word of God we know only from the Scripture adopted by Church proclamation or the proclamation of the Church based on Scripture.

> The written Word of God we know only through the revelation which fulfills proclamation or through the proclamation fulfilled by revelation.

> The preached Word of God we know only through the revelation attested in Scripture or the Scripture which attests revelation.[22]

In this way Barth sought to give due recognition to the otherness of God and the dynamic character of revelation, while at the same time showing that revelation has an objective, knowable content. Barth believed that "We can certainly say what God's Word is, but we must say it indirectly. We must remember the forms in which it is real for us and learn from these forms *how* it is. This How is the attainable human reflection of the unattainable divine What. Our concern must be with this reflection."[23]

Barth's teaching contains important insights into the personal, dynamic, and verbal character of revelation.[24] But is revelation wholly confined to the Word? In reaction to theologies of the Word (whether they be Bultmann's or Barth's), Wolfhart Pannenberg has sought to deemphasize verbal revelation and to ground revelation in history. For Pannenberg history is the outworking of God's actions in human affairs. It is through history that we are able to know God. In bringing the people of Israel out of Egypt and giving them the Promised Land, God "has proved himself to be *their* God, for he has acted on *their* behalf. The exodus and the occupancy of the land are established as the decisive factor in the knowledge of God, and this is so stated in Hosea and later in Jeremiah."[25] Such saving history is not confined to the exodus and the settlement of Israel in the Promised Land. When seen within the framework of prophetic and apocalyptic expectation, the earthly activity of Jesus and his resurrection may be understood as "a reflection of the self-vindication of Jahweh."[26]

In the jargon of theological vocabulary the German word *Heilsgeschichte* became a favorite term in the 1950s and 1960s. Literally it means "history of salvation." We could equally well speak of "salvation history," the "history of redemption," the "history of God's saving acts," or even "sacred history."[27] In dealing with salvation history Pannenberg has a number of concerns. He rightly protests against having double standards. We should not have one set of standards in dealing with sacred history and another set of standards in dealing with secular history. We need the same rigor in dealing with both. This is not only because religious history cannot be treated in a looser fashion. It also has to do with the fact that what we call salvation history cannot be isolated from the rest of history. It forms part of the all-encompassing universal history of the world. Indeed, salvation history claims to provide the key to world history.

Another problem exercises Pannenberg's mind. It has to do with the ambiguity of events. The problem can be put like this. If we see only part of a film on television or in a movie theater, we might be able to work out what happened before we came in. But if we leave before the end, how do we know how it will all work out? Events that happen in the middle of a story cannot be fully understood and appreciated until their significance is shown in the light of subsequent events. For Pannenberg this is true not only of the things that happen in world history; it is also true of the events described in the Bible. People who lived in Old Testament times had insights into the ways of God and through prophecy received glimpses into God's future purposes, but they could not know or grasp precisely what would take place. Nor could they perceive the full significance of events that were happening all around them. The same is true of people who saw and heard Jesus. As Pannenberg puts it, "Revelation is not comprehended completely in the beginning, but at the end of the revealing history."[28]

From our present vantage point in time we cannot see the whole of history. The full revelation of God will come only at the end. Pannenberg believes that his understanding of history corresponds not only to the truth of the nineteenth-century philosopher Hegel's insight into the dynamic of history but is also in line with the broadening perspective of the biblical writers themselves, especially those in the apocalyptic tradition who were concerned with visions of the end time.

The destiny of humankind, from creation onward, is seen to be unfolding according to a divine plan. Apocalyptic thought conceives of a universal history. Thus the revelation of God and his glory is transferred to the end of all events. That the end will make manifest the secrets of the present is also the presupposition of primitive Christianity.

The history that demonstrates the deity of God is broadened to include the totality of all events. This corresponds completely to the universality of Israel's God, who is not only the God of Israel but will be the God of all people. This broadening of the *Heilsgeschichte* to a universal history is in essence already accomplished in the major prophets of Israel in that they treat the kingdoms of the world as responsible to God's commands.[29] With the exception of the lists in Chronicles, this point of view is first carried through systematically in apocalyptic literature. Since the time of the Deuteronomist and the prophets of the Exile, the God of Israel was known as the Lord of all. Correspondingly, the apocalyptic viewpoint conceived of Yahweh's law as the ground of world events. It is at the end of this chain of world events that God can for the first time be revealed with finality as the one true God.[30]

For Pannenberg "the historical revelation is open to anyone who has eyes to see. It has a universal character."[31] It is no gnostic secret shared only by a select band of initiates. But this does not mean that all events are equally revealing. Rather, the history of Israel consists of a series of special events that "communicate something special which could not be gotten out

of other events. This special aspect is the event itself, not the
attitude with which one confronts the event."[32] Faith is not
something that can leap over the gap between the believer and
the historical fact by serving as a substitute for the latter.[33]

> Faith has to do with the future. This is the essence of trust. Trust
> primarily directs itself toward the future, and the future justifies, or
> disappoints. Thus a person does not come to faith blindly, but by
> means of an event that can be appropriated as something that can
> be considered reliable. True faith is not a state of blissful gullibility.
> The prophets could call Israel to faith in Jahweh's promises and
> proclaim his prophecy because Israel had experienced the depend-
> ability of their God in the course of a long history. The Christian
> risks his trust, life, and future on the fact of God's having been
> revealed in the fate of Jesus. . . . The proclamation of the gospel
> cannot assert that the facts are in doubt and that the leap of faith
> must be made in order to achieve certainty. If this sort of assertion
> were allowed to stand, then one would have to cease being a
> theologian and Christian. The proclamation must assert that the
> facts are reliable and that you can therefore place your faith, life,
> and future on them.[34]

From here Pannenberg goes on to argue that "the universal
revelation of the deity of God is not yet realized in the history of
Israel, but first in the fate of Jesus of Nazareth, insofar as the
end of all events is anticipated in his fate."[35] We noted earlier
how Pannenberg regards the resurrection of Jesus as a historical
event.[36] It is also the historical event that illuminates the rest of
history and anticipates the end of history and the eschatological
manifestation of God.

> With the resurrection of Jesus, the end of history has already
> occurred, although it does not strike us in this way. It is through the
> resurrection that the God of Israel has substantiated his deity in an
> ultimate way and is now manifest as the God of all men. It is only
> the eschatological character of the Christ event that establishes that
> there will be no further self-manifestation of God beyond this event.
> Thus, the end of the world will be on a cosmic scale what has
> already happened in Jesus. It is the eschatological character of the
> Christ event as the anticipation of the end of all things that alone
> can establish this development so that from now on the non-Jew
> can acknowledge the God of Israel as the one true God, the one
> whom Greek philosophy sought and the only one who could be
> acknowledged as the one true God from that time on.[37]

What then is the relationship between revelation–history
and what Scripture presents as "the Word of God"? Pannenberg's reply is that the Word relates itself to revelation as

"foretelling, forthtelling, and report."[38] It foretells in the sense that

> Israel experienced the self-vindication of Jahweh in the given events of history largely as a confirmation of words of promise or threat that are still in the future. Nevertheless, the prophetic word is the vehicle of proclamation and thus is not of itself the self-vindication of God. If it is to be found in visions and auditions, these were not understood as the direct self-disclosure of God.[39]

It forthtells, Pannenberg maintains, in the sense that "the Israelite Law of God presupposed the knowledge of the deity of Jahweh and also his self-vindication as demonstrated. Law and commandment follow as a result of the divine self-vindication. They do not themselves have the character of revelation."[40] The same applies to the declarations of Jesus that are characterized as the Word of God. "The authority of Jesus as the bearer of the authority of God himself is thus already presupposed."[41] The Word of God as proclamation or kerygma appears for the first time in the New Testament.

> The message of the apostles is called the Word of God, because it is decisively set in motion (1 Thess. 2:13) through the appearances of Jesus (Gal. 1:12, 15f.). This is not because of human effort, but because of God himself. . . . The issuing of the kerygma, as the report of the revelation of God in the fate of Jesus, is itself an element in the accomplishment of the revelation event. The self-vindication of God before all men cannot be thought of apart from the universal notification. However, the kerygma is not by itself a revelatory speech by virtue of its formal characteristic, that is, as a challenge or call. The kerygma is to be understood solely on the basis of its content, on the basis of the event that it reports or explicates. In this sense, the kerygma is not to be thought of as bringing something to the event. The events in which God demonstrates his deity are self-evident as they stand within the framework of their own history. It does not require any kind of inspired interpretation to make these events recognizable as revelation.[42]

Some students of biblical theology feel that Pannenberg falls into that category of men whom Coleridge described as being mostly right in what they affirm and wrong in what they deny. After all, the positive commitment to revelation in history does not depend on denial of God's self-disclosure through spoken or written word. But is Pannenberg really saying this? To adapt Pannenberg's own language, insofar as history is related to the Word of promise it is an extension of that Word, and insofar as the Word proclaims revelation—history it is an extension of that history. Or as Conzelmann puts it with reference to Romans 1:16–17, "The historical saving event is actualized in the word."[43] It is the concrete means by which past history is known and appropriated in the present. To use the language that we used earlier in describing what the historian achieves, the Word presents us with a model or series of models that enable us to grasp the reality it describes.

This is not the place to discuss Pannenberg's inclination to see the influence of Gnosticism in early Christian thought about revelation. Pannenberg himself draws attention to fundamental differences between the biblical and gnostic outlook.[44] The evidence for Gnosticism proper is in any case later than the New Testament period. More serious is Pannenberg's apparent double assumption that revelation is to be thought of in general terms rather than in personal and individual ones, and that words and utterances have some kind of secondary status in history. On the one hand, his discussion of revelation tends to focus on public events to the exclusion of what happens between God and the individual. And on the other hand, he seems to overlook the fact that an utterance can be no less historically significant than an act. Indeed, most historical events are combinations of acts and utterances.

It is not only "performative utterances" that have an event-like character, although some biblical utterances appear to belong to this category.[45] The words of Jesus were not something secondary to his ministry and "fate" but part and parcel of them. As Joachim Jeremias observes with regard to Jesus' proclamation of the kingdom, "The return of the spirit of God is manifested not only in actions, but also in words of authority."[46] It would seem odd to deny a revelatory role to the parables. This is not to say that they must be understood as communicating propositions that could not otherwise be known. The communication of propositions is an important function of language, but it is only one of its functions. The parables work by bringing the hearer to the point of seeing himself in the light of an eschatology that is "in process of realization" and of acting accordingly.[47] They take the form of a language-event that brings about a disclosure situation[48] in which existence is seen in relation to God. To see our existence in relation to God is of the essence of revelation.[49]

A point to be underlined is that such a disclosure can take place through reflection on history (both in the sense of events and accounts of events) and through reflection on words that have no immediate connection with history at all. It is the occupational hazard of the theologian who has important insights to overstate his case. Barth did this when he so stressed revelation through the Word that he felt obligated to deny any revelation in nature.[50] It would be equally wrong to treat history and language as mutually exclusive media of revelation. One of the great theological needs today is for a coherent account of revelation as it occurs in the Word, in history, in nature, and in experience.

In the past, Evangelicals have sometimes lapsed into a way of speaking about the Bible as the Word of God that gave the impression of a monophysitism in which the divine absorbed the human. Just as in a docetic christology Jesus only appears to be a man but is not one really, so the humanity of the Bible has been treated merely as the superficial clothing of what is essentially divine. No doubt this is all part of a reaction against the liberalism that went to the opposite extreme of seeing the Bible as a collection of purely human writings that reflect certain phases of the history of Middle-Eastern religion. But this liberal understanding of Scripture is at variance not only with the claims of the biblical writings themselves but also with the attitude of Jesus toward the Scriptures and with their revelatory role in Christian experience.[51] The study of the christological controversies of the early church shows that truth was not served either by coming down in favor of one extreme to the exclusion of the other or by seeking a middle-course compromise. What is required in our contemporary understanding of revelation is recognition of both the divine and human elements together. Because revelation is a historical revelation in word and event, it is to be understood precisely in its historicity. Whatever means are appropriate to the understanding of it in its historicity are therefore to be used. At the same time, any approach that does not understand it in its revelatory aspect falls short of understanding it as a historical reality.

There is a second and kindred danger to which Christians are prone in speaking of Scripture as the Word of God. That is to confine revelation merely to the verbatim pronouncements of the text. But to accept this would mean, for example, that in preaching, revelation takes place only when texts of Scripture are actually quoted. The logical conclusion would be that sermons (or for that matter, any form of Christian witness) should consist of nothing but a compilation of texts. In its extreme form it would give the Bible a quasi-magical character, making it operate regardless of our faculties of cognition and understanding, merely by the performance of the appropriate act.

But this is not the view of the biblical writers themselves.

There is a sense in which for them the whole of life and reality is sacramental.[52] Natural events and human actions, while still remaining natural events and human actions, point beyond themselves and have a significance that is wider than the dimensions of time and space. In so doing, they bring God right into the midst of life. "The heavens declare the glory of God; the skies proclaim the work of his hands," the psalmist wrote (Ps. 19:1). Paul argued that all human beings are responsible before God, "since what may be known about God is plain to them, because God has made it plain to them. For since the creation of the world God's invisible qualities—his eternal power and divine nature—have been clearly seen, being understood from what has been made, so that men are without excuse" (Rom. 1:19–20). The same basic view is presented in the accounts of Paul's preaching in Acts 14:17 and 17:26–28. In the latter passage Paul alludes to pagan Greek writers who have genuine insights into God's nature. For Paul this knowledge of God which human beings have as creatures is the reason why they are accountable to God. The physical world mediates an ongoing awareness and understanding of God. It is through the world that creatures stand in a relation to God.

Similarly, an act of sin is like an inverted sacrament. It affects not only our fellow human beings on a human plane but also our relationship with God. In 1 John 4:12 we read that "no one has ever seen God; but if we love each other, God lives in us and his love is made complete in us." Although we have not seen God directly, God's presence is realized through love of other human beings. In a sense sin is the opposite of this. Through alienation from others we are alienated from God. Matthew 25 depicts the judgment of the nations by the Son of Man. It will be like a shepherd's separation of sheep from the goats. The decisive factor in the condemnation of the unrighteous is their failure to meet the needs of the stranger, the naked, the sick, and the prisoner, and thus failure to serve the Son of Man. Conversely, the King will say to the righteous who had done these things, "I tell you the truth, whatever you did for one of the least of these brothers of mine, you did for me" (Matt. 25:40).

The parable suggests that not all such situations are revelatory at the time. For the righteous may well be unaware of what they were doing. Similarly, the unrighteous protest that they never saw the Son of Man in these situations. There is in life a kind of divine incognito which turns out to be a revelation only in retrospect. In saying this we are brought back to the point made early on in the discussion of Kierkegaard: while historical events can be described in secular terms, the same events can also be seen in relation to God. Earlier I suggested that in this process the believer interprets events and actions in the light of other events and actions.[53] One of the purposes of the parable of Matthew 25 is to teach disciples to see ordinary, secular events and situations from God's perspective.

John Hick has called attention to the interpretative aspect of faith. The discovery of God is not like finding a new fact. It arises from "interpreting in a new way what was already before us. It is epistemologically comparable, not to the discovery of a man concealed behind a screen, or of inferred electrons underlying the observed behavior of matter, but to what Wittgenstein called 'seeing as.'"[54] As Hick goes on to illustrate, when the Chaldeans were at the gates of Jerusalem, the prophet Jeremiah experienced the event not simply as a foreign political threat but also as God's judgment on Israel.

This act of "seeing as" or "experiencing as" may operate at different levels and in different areas of experience. A primitive man who finds a piece of paper covered with writing may interpret it as something made by man. A more educated man may realize that it is something written in a foreign language. A person who knows that language may be able to read it. An expert may be able to understand its significance. Thus each of these people may answer the question "What is it?" correctly but at different levels. Each of the more adequate attributions of significance presupposes the less adequate ones. As Hick observes, "The significance of an object to an individual consists in the practical difference which that object makes to him, the way in which it affects either his immediate reactions or his more long-term plans and policies."[55]

Broadly speaking, there are three main levels of significance: the physical world, the human world, and the world in relation to God. Both within these three levels and between them there is a kind of reciprocal action in our interpretation. We approach new items of knowledge with an existing framework of knowledge and interpretation. The primitive man may recognize the piece of paper to be the work of a man because he already has some idea of the works of nature and of the works of men. The expert, likewise, is able to interpret the paper because he already knows something of the language and of the kind of thing indicated by the writing on it. But the new experience in turn adds to or modifies previous experience and thus also modifies the existing framework of knowledge and interpretation.

My contention is that all experience (and with it, of course, history) is in principle capable of being revelatory. This is not to say that we see the significance of it at the time or even that we shall necessarily come to see the revelatory significance of any particular event. Rather, it is to say that events are in principle capable of being understood at the three levels of significance just noted: at the levels of nature, humanity, and in relation to God. It is on this last level that revelation, in the Christian sense, takes place. When we see the significance of an event as disclosing something about our relationship with God, and with each other in relation to God, revelation takes place. Whether we see significance at any of these levels depends on the interplay between the individual, the event or thing in question, and the individual's frame of reference. When there is obscurity in any of these factors, the significance will be correspondingly obscure. This may be due to a variety of factors, such as lack of knowledge, inadequate perception, being content with inadequate explanations, or an inadequate frame of reference. These factors operate at all levels of significance, no less on the level of revelation than in the study of nature and history. But in revelation, history comes in at two points. It is the raw material or medium of revelation. And it also forms an essential part of the frame of reference by which that raw material is interpreted.

The Importance of History for Faith

The contemporary cultural and intellectual climate has encouraged numerous attempts to cut faith loose from history. Some people see faith as a purely personal affair. The anti-intellectual person cannot be bothered with arguments about history. Those who are committed to social programs often feel that history is an esoteric concern which just sidetracks people from the real issues. The skeptic suspects that historical research undermines the fabric of belief by showing that faith is not supported by the facts of history. Philosophers in the tradition of logical positivism have argued that religious language is largely meaningless. It lacks intelligible content. Its chief function is to express the hopes, fears, and values of the individual and the community to which he or she belongs.

The first half of the twentieth century saw an aggressive, skeptical hostility to religion which treated various faiths as obsolete relics of bygone ages. Now, however, the former intolerance seems to have been replaced by a benign indifference which sees some social value in the practice of religion but remains skeptical about religious truth claims. One indication of the changing mood was R. B. Braithwaite's celebrated Eddington Memorial Lecture for 1955, *An Empiricist's View of the Nature of Religious Belief*. Braithwaite was a distinguished philosopher of science at Cambridge University. He was influenced by logical positivism, but he was also aware of its shortcomings. Braithwaite claimed that "a man is not, I think, a professing Christian unless he both proposes to live according to Christian moral principles and associates his intention with thinking of Christian stories; but he need not believe that the empirical propositions presented by these stories correspond to empirical fact."[56] We may accept the first of these propositions, but the second does not necessarily follow. Underlying Braithwaite's view is the contention that such stories are not empirically verifiable, but what can be verified is the way in which they are used. On his analysis, the Christian's assertion that God is love, which Braithwaite takes "to epitomize the assertions of the Christian religion," is reduced to a declaration of "his intention to follow an agapeistic way of life."[57]

If Braithwaite means that God is not a term capable of historical explanation in that God is not a historical figure like Napoleon or Julius Caesar, the point is true but relatively trivial. We have gone further and said with Kierkegaard that there is a sense in which in history God is incognito. He is not seen directly even in the figure of Jesus Christ for much of his life. We have also argued that historical explanations (whether or not we bring God into them) are not literal descriptions of certain empirical facts but are hypotheses or models that help to identify, join together, explain, and put constructions on empirical facts. They are validated by being put together in a way that seems best to fit these facts and to make a coherent explanation. Such explanations may be given at different levels, depending on the frame of reference or level of significance. A secular explanation is possible and valid within a secular frame of reference, but it may not be exhaustive. If there is something in history that bursts this frame of reference (such as the resurrection of Jesus), we are justified in seeking a wider one. This in turn means that our frame of reference for looking at other events at their deeper levels of significance will be wider.

Insofar as historical propositions are expressed in language, we may agree with Braithwaite that our understanding of these propositions must be determined by the way in which they are used and that this is a matter of empirical investigation. But we take issue with him over the suggestion that it is immaterial in what sense the Christian stories are true. The propositions associated with the stories of Christian origins take a variety of forms. Some are expressly parabolic. If they are about conduct and attitudes in a more general sense (like the parable of the Good Samaritan), their truth does not depend on the demonstration of the historicity of a unique event. On the other hand, a parable may have bearing on the historical claims of Jesus, showing that the messianic age has arrived in the person of Jesus.[58] In such a case, the truth and bearing of the parable are bound up with the historical validity of those claims. So too is the response demanded by the parable. If an event such as the Exodus is seen as a paradigm of God's care for his people,[59] the comfort and hope that the believer is exhorted to draw from it are surely ill founded if there is no corresponding historical base. Similarly, the Christian hope for the future and the Christian understanding of history are grounded in the historicity of the resurrection of Jesus. "If Christ has not been raised, our preaching is useless and so is your faith" (1 Cor. 15:14).

Does this then mean that faith must always be at the mercy of the historian and critical expert? The American liberal theologian John Knox has replied in the negative.[60] So too, despite (or because of) its skepticism, has the Bultmann school.[61] An answer more in line with the convictions of the biblical writers themselves is that of Walter Künneth: "Revelation is . . . always more than history, not only history, but not without history."[62] If our faith is of the kind that would persist regardless of evidence and regardless of historical models, it is an unanchored faith. Its utterances might be indicative of the believer's particular mental states, but they would not be informative about anything that is the case outside them. If it could be shown that, say, the gospel accounts of Jesus were without historical foundation in his life,[63] it is conceivable that I could go on having religious experiences, but the explanation of them would be different. I would have to look beyond the Christian explanation.

For the Christian the question of "belief in" is inseparable from the question of "belief that." It is precisely the Christian's belief that God has acted in certain ways in history that determines his belief about the character of God and the destiny of the world. We might echo the words of R. P. C. Hanson, "If we ignore the significance of history, we leave the field open to the fanatic, the fraud and the fool."[64] But if we reflect on the character of the Bible, it is not a kind of promise box or a means of administering a kind of spiritual LSD that sends people on "trips." In fact, it is full of arguments, demonstrations, appeals to history, and interpretations of history. Examples are the prologue of Luke's gospel with its stress on the historicity of the story of Jesus as the basis of faith and 1 Corinthians 15:1ff., where Paul stresses the historical foundation of his preaching. It is on the basis of such arguments that the validity of Christian faith rests. The ordinary believer is not required to work out all the arguments for himself any more than the average motorist needs to understand the scientific basis of the working of his car. Nor, indeed, need every item of belief be demonstrably true. It is legitimate to accept with integrity unverified assertions on the basis of the credit and authority of the person who makes them, but it is important to be able to establish that credit.

In one sense my argument has been a negative one. I have been arguing that history could conceivably undermine the foundations of Christian faith if historians were to show that Christian beliefs about history were ill founded. To put it on its lowest level, history is important because of the truth claims of Christianity. But there is another side to the coin. History has a positive role to play. The better we understand biblical history and the subsequent history of the church, the better will be our position for understanding what Christianity is really about. A person's faith can be strengthened not only by being assured that it rests on a solid foundation, but by having a more accurate and deeper appreciation of people, situations, and events.

We all have beliefs about the past that have been arrived at consciously or unconsciously, critically or uncritically. The historical models that we make in our minds for understanding the past may be crude and inaccurate, but we cannot help making them. It is the job of the expert—whether he be a professional historian or, in the case of Christian belief, a minister and teacher—to show what is wrong with the misleading models and to help build more accurate ones and to interpret them correctly. But without the models we cannot grasp the reality they signify, and in the end each of us is responsible for what we make of them. In that sense, we all must be our own historians.

A Note on the Gospel Miracles

Early in the present century Reinhold Seeberg observed that miracles were once the foundation of all apologetics. Later they became an apologetic crutch, and in modern times they are often regarded as a cross for apologetics to bear.[1] Like all aphorisms this verdict contains a measure of exaggeration and oversimplification. But it also contains a measure of truth. For many people today miracles are an embarrassment. They would feel more comfortable with the Bible if the miracle stories had been omitted.

In chapter 1 we looked at some of the problems presented by miracles. Can the gospel miracles be taken seriously as history? In former times miracles were regarded as part of the credentials of Christianity. They provided supernatural attestation for its truth claims. But if the events themselves are historically doubtful, what happens to the truth claims? With the rise of critical thinking, people have been inclined to advocate the truth of Christianity on grounds other than miracles. Many scholars downplay the miracle stories, while others deny them outright. At the turn of the century the History of Religions School sought to interpret Christianity in the context of the evolution of religion. A leading spokesman of this school was Wilhelm Bousset. In his book *Kyrios Christos* (1913) Bousset argued that Jesus was not really a miracle worker at all.[2] The miracle stories were really late accretions to the gospel tradition which had their origin in the Hellenistic world. "People transferred to Jesus all sorts of stories which were current about this or that wonder worker and decorated gospel narratives that were already at hand with current miraculous motifs."[3]

For some time it has been fashionable to compare the gospel picture of Jesus with wonder-working "divine men"[4] in the ancient world. Some have suggested that Jesus was really just another "divine man" with no more claims to divinity than other holy men in antiquity. Others have argued that the Gospels were really trying to combat a tendency in early Christianity to make Jesus into a wonder-working "divine man." The Gospels' emphasis on suffering and the Cross is itself a counterbalance to the tendency to turn the message about Jesus into a celebration of pure power and triumph.

More recently, Morton Smith, in his book *Jesus the Magician*[5] (1978), has argued that the New Testament account of Jesus is really a massive cover-up operation that deliberately conceals the true identity of Jesus. Professor Smith argues that Jesus really was a magician and that his "miracles" were acts of sorcery. If this is so, then clearly the whole credibility of Christianity is called into question.

I have examined these ideas in some detail in my book *Miracles and the Critical Mind*. The reader who is interested in pursuing this question will find there my response to these and other ideas, together with details of scholarly literature examining the ramifications of the question. The purpose of this note is to draw attention to some features of the gospel accounts of the miracles of Jesus that appear to have been largely neglected, but which have bearing on the question of the underlying historicity of the miracles and the identity of Jesus. The argument is developed more fully in *Miracles and the Critical Mind*, chapter 11; in *That You May Believe*, chapters 7–11; and in my article "Synoptic Miracle Stories: A Jewish Religious and Social Setting."[6]

My point turns on Jewish attitudes toward miracles. If we look at Jewish writings about miracles we find a curious but significant ambivalence. The ancient rabbis accepted them but steadfastly refused to draw any theological conclusions from them. Talmudic literature preserves a number of miracle stories. Underlying this ambivalent attitude is the firm Jewish belief that the Torah (or Law, as it is frequently termed) contains the Word of the Lord. As such, it gives the basic guidance and instruction that human beings need. No miracle, however impressive, may serve to validate any teaching. Indeed, a sign or wonder used to validate teaching that conflicts with the Torah is *ipso facto* to be treated as the work of a false prophet.

This position has its roots in the Torah itself. Deuteronomy 13:1–5 lays down the attitude that should be taken toward prophets who lead people astray by false teaching supported by miraculous signs and wonders.

If a prophet, or one who foretells by dreams, appears among you
and announces to you a miraculous sign or wonder, and if the sign
or wonder of which he has spoken takes place, and he says, "Let us
follow other gods" (gods you have not known) "and let us worship
them," you must not listen to the words of that prophet or dreamer.
The LORD your God is testing you to find out whether you love him
with all your heart and with all your soul. It is the LORD your God
you must follow, and him you must revere. Keep his commands
and obey him; serve him and hold fast to him. That prophet or
dreamer must be put to death, because he preached rebellion
against the LORD your God, who brought you out of Egypt and
redeemed you from the land of slavery; he has tried to turn you
from the way the LORD your God commanded you to follow. You
must purge the evil from among you.

Thus the people of Israel should treat such miracles as tests
of their allegiance to the Lord. Not only should the prophet be
disregarded; the rebellious prophet should be killed, so that the
evil may be purged from the midst of the people. The passage
goes on to warn against the danger of leading astray a whole
town (Deut. 13:13). When this happens, the whole town is to be
destroyed, though only after diligent inquiry has produced
proof that "this detestable thing has been done among you"
(v. 14).

Deuteronomy 13 has long been familiar in theological debate.
Calvin appealed to it in dealing with reports of Roman Catholic
miracles.[7] When Catholics appealed to miracles in their church
to show that it was still the true church, Calvin argued that
such miracles were like those described in Deuteronomy 13.
They could not be used to support Catholic truth claims. B. B.
Warfield appealed to this passage in rejecting the miracles of
Lourdes. No event that had "implications inconsistent with
fundamental religious truth" could be regarded as a divine
miracle.[8]

This passage from Deuteronomy has a significance that
reaches beyond apologetics and modern discussions of miraculous phenomena. It provides us with an essential clue to
understanding the attitudes of the Jewish religious leaders
toward Jesus. When the Jewish authorities found Jesus profan-
ing the sabbath, teaching a different understanding of the
Torah from theirs, assuming an authority which they believed
no man had the right to assume, performing signs and
wonders, and attracting a following, they naturally asked
themselves what they should do about him. Being devout Jews,
they turned to the Torah for guidance. They found their answer
in Deuteronomy 13 and other passages dealing with rebellion,

abominable practices, sorcery, and leading the people astray.[9] Having convinced themselves that Jesus was the kind of person described in Deuteronomy 13, they came to the conclusion that they had only one option: the evildoer must be purged from the midst of the people.

This explanation helps us to make sense of the events described in Mark 3 and the parallel passages in Matthew 12 and Luke 6 and 11. Mark has already told how from the outset of his public ministry Jesus cast out demons and healed people. Mark 2 tells of Jesus healing the paralytic through pronouncing the forgiveness of his sins. The scribes treat this as blasphemy, but the people are repeatedly amazed at Jesus' teaching. The growing differences with the Pharisees lead to a dispute over the lawfulness of the disciples' action in plucking grain on the Sabbath. Matters come to a head with the Sabbath-day healing of the man with the withered hand in the synagogue at Capernaum. Mark records that the event prompted the Pharisees to take counsel with the Herodians on how to destroy Jesus (Mark 3:6; cf. Matt. 12:14; Luke 6:11).

Jesus withdraws, but the crowds follow him, and he continues his ministry of healing and exorcism. The disciples are commissioned to preach and cast out demons. On returning home he is accused by scribes from Jerusalem of being possessed by Beelzebul, i.e., Satan (Mark 3:22; cf. Matt. 9:34; 12:24; Luke 11:15). The charge, which is bound up with the decision to destroy Jesus, is evidently the outcome of the growing conviction that Jesus is an evildoer, and it ascribes Jesus' healing work to the activity of Satan. Jesus meets the charge by pointing out its self-contradictory character. "How can Satan drive out Satan?" "If Satan opposes himself and is divided, he cannot stand; his end has come." Jesus then issues a stern warning: "I tell you the truth, all the sins and blasphemies of men will be forgiven them. But whoever blasphemes against the Holy Spirit will never be forgiven; he is guilty of an eternal sin" (Mark 3:28–29; cf. Matt. 12:31–32; Luke 12:10).

Mark brings out the significance of this warning in his comment, "He said this because they were saying, 'He has an evil spirit'" (Mark 3:30). In other words, blasphemy against the Holy Spirit—the ultimate blasphemy—is to attribute the work of the Holy Spirit to Satan. Jesus' opponents were identifying with Satan the Spirit which anointed Jesus as the messianic Son of God following his baptism (cf. Matt. 3:13–17; Mark 1:9–11; Luke 3:21–11; John 1:29–34), and they also were attributing Jesus' healings to Satan. The Evangelists attribute Jesus' healings to the Holy Spirit (cf. Matt. 12:18, 28; Luke 4:14, 18; 11:20) and to the Father (John 5:36; 8:28; 10:37–38; 14:10–11; 17:4, 21).

John's gospel does not use the name Beelzebul, but it records the damning charge that Jesus is a Samaritan and has a demon (John 8:48, 52; cf. 7:20; 10:20). Perhaps the idea that Jesus was a Samaritan was linked with the perception that Jesus was teaching a deviant form of religion. It may also be bound up with the fact that Jesus spent some time in Samaria and was associated with Samaritans (John 4:9; 39–40). In any event, the charge was linked with attempts to kill Jesus on the grounds that he was leading the people astray (John 7:20, 25; 8:59; 10:33). The high priest Caiaphas justified to the Sanhedrin the death of Jesus as an act of expediency. It would avert the national disaster that would come about if the people were led astray by Jesus' many signs (John 11:47–53).

It would take us too far afield to examine particular miracle stories in detail, but certain further observations are relevant to the argument. From what has been said so far it is clear that the synoptic Gospels and John converge in their presentation of the Jewish leaders' opposition to Jesus. Jesus' miracles are seen as satanic or demonic with the potential for leading the people astray. Initially the fears may have been localized. It may well be, as Ethelbert Stauffer has suggested, that Capernaum would become a "seduced city" in view of the fact that Jesus' activity was centered on Capernaum.[10] This would explain the presence of Torah lawyers from Jerusalem (Mark 3:22 and parallels noted above). They concluded that Jesus was indeed casting out demons and that he was leading people astray. Because he was doing both of these things, he must be satanic. The ground was thus prepared for the condemnation and extermination of Jesus.

The charge that Jesus was possessed by Satan failed to stick. Jesus showed its self-contradictory character. But this was not the end of the matter, for the charge was followed by a request for a sign (Matt. 12:38; 16:1; Mark 8:11; Luke 11:16; cf. John 6:30). It may be, as is frequently assumed, that the request was motivated by a desire for a clear-cut sign that would have established beyond all doubt that Jesus was doing the works of God. On the other hand, if Jesus had performed a sign, especially a nature miracle like the feeding of the multitudes that Mark has just described, Jesus' opponents would have had clear-cut evidence, attested by impeccable witnesses, i.e., themselves, that they could use to support their claim that Jesus was a wonder-working magician. Matthew and Luke not only record Jesus' refusal to perform a sign on demand, but they go on to record the saying about the sign of Jonah. The sign of Jonah was not like other prophetic signs, including the sort of sign that Jesus was requested to perform. Such signs were done by the prophet. The sign of Jonah was a sign that was done *to* the prophet. The Old Testament Book of Jonah describes how Jonah was cast into the sea as an evildoer whose actions had caused a storm. However, God came to his rescue by restoring his life. The saying about the sign of Jonah in effect says that Jesus' opponents will have a hand in bringing about the sign. They will judge Jesus as an evildoer, but God will restore Jesus and so reverse their verdict.

The procedure laid down in Deuteronomy 13 for dealing with prophets who lead astray by means of signs and wonders finds further echoes in the Gospels and in postbiblical Judaism. Deuteronomy 13:3 treats the appearance of such a prophet as a test to see whether the people love the Lord their God with all their heart and soul. The gospel accounts of the discussions with Jesus over the Great Commandment may well have had as their motive the desire to test Jesus' orthodoxy on that score (cf. Matt. 22:34–40; Mark 12:28–34; Luke 10:25–28; 20:39–40). Jesus' reply not only endorsed the teaching of Deuteronomy 6:5 and 13:3–4 but linked with it the command of Leviticus 19:18 to love one's neighbor. When seen in this light, Jesus' signs did not lead people astray but rather exemplified the two great commandments upon which hang all the Law and the Prophets.

In Matthew 24:24 and Mark 13:22 explicit reference is made to Deuteronomy 13. But here the argument is turned around. Jesus himself warns against the false Christs and false prophets who would lead astray the elect, if it were possible, through performing signs and wonders. When we turn to the gospel accounts of Jesus' trial and execution we find further hints that he was thought to be a wonder-working, false prophet who led people astray. The high priest adjured Jesus in language evocative of exorcism (Matt. 26:63). Jesus was mockingly invited to prophesy (Matt. 26:68; Mark 14:65; Luke 22:64) and to save himself by a miracle (Matt. 27:42–43; Mark 15:31–32; Luke 23:35). The guard at the tomb described Jesus as "that deceiver" who prophesied his own resurrection (Matt. 27:63).

When we turn to postbiblical Judaism we find that the teaching of Deuteronomy continues to play a decisive part in dealing with false prophets who lead the people astray. The Mishnah tractate Sanhedrin prescribes death for blasphemers, idolaters, profaners of the Sabbath, those who lead towns astray, sorcerers, and stubborn rebellious sons (Sanhedrin 7:4, 8). Sanhedrin 10:4 explicitly refers to Deuteronomy 13:13 in dealing with "beguilers" of a city and discusses the circumstances under which they are to be put to death. The tradition that Jesus was a sorcerer who led Israel astray is preserved in the Babylonian Talmud, though in a garbled form (Sanhedrin 43a). A somewhat earlier testimony to the same basic Jewish view of Jesus comes from the pen of the Christian apologist Justin Martyr, who describes the Jewish view of Christianity as "a godless and lawless heresy . . . sprung from one Jesus, a Galilaean deceiver, whom we crucified, but his disciples stole him by night from the tomb."[11]

What is the significance of all this? Several points stand out. To begin with, we have to recognize that we cannot separate the teaching of Jesus from his activity as an exorcist, healer, and worker of signs and wonders. It was precisely the combination of Jesus' teaching and wonder-working activity that provoked the conflict with the Jewish authorities. Jewish tradition tells of holy men like Honi the Circle Drawer and Hanina ben Dosa.[12] Sundry miracles were associated with such men. But what distinguishes them from Jesus is that they did not set themselves up as teachers or prophets. They taught no new doctrine, nor did they deviate from the accepted interpretations of the Law. The wonders associated with them were seen as the answers of God to the prayers and piety of holy men. The issue is not whether Jesus simply was a magician or not,[13] but whether he was a deceiver who used signs and wonders to lead the people astray.

The liberal picture of Jesus as simply an enlightened, humanitarian religious teacher is a figment of the imagination. Jesus the teacher cannot be separated from Jesus the healer, exorcist, and wonder worker. The claim that Jesus was a healer, exorcist, and wonder worker is not based simply on the gospel accounts of particular miracles. It is, in fact, implicit in the opposition to Jesus by the Pharisees, scribes, and Jewish religious leaders.

If this is so, we cannot treat the miracles of Jesus (as Bousset and others have done) as late additions to the traditions about Jesus which were modeled on stories from the Greek and Roman world. It is not as if the original historical Jesus was a holy and wise teacher who was later turned into a miracle worker. It is not as if the early church found it necessary to improve the image of Jesus by inventing miracle stories. Rather, the Jewish opposition to Jesus was rooted in the fact that he was perceived to be from the very beginning a worker of signs and wonders that were bound up with his teaching and claims to authority. This argument does not, of course, demonstrate the historicity of each and every miracle story in the Gospels. That is not its point. It does, however, indicate that Jesus was perceived by his opponents to have been some kind of prophetic wonder worker. The fact that his opponents saw him in this way provides impressive additional testimony to Christian claims about Jesus. Thus the issue shifts from that of whether Jesus was a wonder worker or not to the question of the power by which Jesus did things. In the eyes of his opponents Jesus' powers were evil and satanic. In the eyes of the gospel writers Jesus was the messianic Son of God who was anointed by the Holy Spirit to do the redemptive work of the Father.

In the apologetic of the New Testament writers the resurrection of Jesus is treated rather differently from the way in which some more recent Christian writers treat it. The New Testament writers do not argue that if God could do something so difficult as raising the dead to life, he could easily have performed lesser miracles. Nor do they argue that, since Jesus was divine, he could not remain dead. The emphasis falls on Jesus *being raised* from the dead or on *being raised* by the Father.[14] The resurrection of Jesus means the reversal of the verdict passed on Jesus by the Sanhedrin. The Sanhedrin was the supreme Jewish council. It had both legislative and judiciary authority. Under God it was the highest human authority on earth. In terms of the Jewish law the only construction that could be placed on the death of Jesus was that he was under the curse of God (Gal. 3:13; cf. Deut. 21:23). The slogan "Jesus be cursed" (1 Cor. 12:3) may well represent the official Jewish attitude on how orthodox Jews should regard Jesus. Jesus was condemned as a blasphemer with messianic pretensions who was seeking to lead the people astray (Matt. 26:63–66; Mark 14:64–65; Luke 22:66–23:3; John 11:47–53). But if Jesus was raised from the dead, the verdict of the highest human court was overturned by the highest authority of all. The resurrection of Jesus is the ground of the Christian hope in eternal life. It is also the vindication of Jesus, showing that his works were not (as his opponents claimed) Satanic works but the very works of God himself.

Notes

Preface

[1] Downers Grove and Leicester: InterVarsity, 1975. The other three studies were by Gordon Wenham, "History and the Old Testament"; F. F. Bruce, "Myth and History"; and R. T. France, "The Authenticity of the Sayings of Jesus." A French translation was published under the title *Verité Historique et Critique Biblique* (Lausanne: Presses Bibliques Universitaires, 1982).

[2] Among these mention may be made of George E. Marsden and Frank Roberts, eds., *A Christian View of History?* (Grand Rapids: Eerdmans, 1975); Langdon Gilkey, *Reaping the Whirlwind: A Christian Interpretation of History* (New York: Seabury, 1976); Herbert Butterfield, *Writings on Christianity and History*, ed. with an introduction by C. T. McIntire (New York: Oxford University Press, 1979); C. T. McIntire, ed., *God, History and Historians* (New York: Oxford University Press, 1977); A. E. Harvey, *Jesus and the Constraints of History*, Bampton Lectures, 1980 (Philadelphia: Westminster; London: SPCK, 1982); C. T. McIntire and Ronald A. Wells, eds., *History and Historical Understanding* (Grand Rapids: Eerdmans, 1984); Gordon E. Michalson, Jr., *Lessing's "Ugly Ditch": A Study of Theology and History* (University Park, Pa., and London: Pennsylvania State University Press, 1985); Ronald H. Nash, *Christian Faith and Historical Understanding* (Grand Rapids: Zondervan, 1984); Dominick La Capra, *History and Criticism* (Ithaca, N.Y., and London: Cornell University Press, 1985); and sundry articles published under the auspices of the Conference on Faith and History in its publication *Fides et Historia*, notably in vols. 13–14 (1981–82).

[3] *Miracles and the Critical Mind* (Grand Rapids: Eerdmans, 1984).

[4] *That You May Believe: Miracles and Faith—Then and Now* (Grand Rapids: Eerdmans, 1985).

Introduction

[1] *Theology of the New Testament*, trans. Kendrick Grobel, 2 vols. (New York: Scribner; London: SCM, 1952–), 1:3. I have examined Bultmann's thought in *Philosophy and the Christian Faith: A Historical Sketch from the Middle Ages to the Present Day* (Downers Grove and Leicester: InterVarsity, 1968, 1985), pp. 185–91; and more fully in "Bultmann Revisited," *The Churchman* 88 (1974): 167–87.

[2] "On the Proof of the Spirit and of Power" (1777), quoted from Henry Chadwick, ed. and trans., *Lessing's Theological Writings* (London: A. & C. Black; Stanford: Stanford University Press, 1956), p. 53. Lessing was replying to critics who objected to his publication of the notorious *Wolfenbüttel Fragments*, which attacked the historical credibility of Christianity. For extracts from Reimarus see *Reimarus: Fragments*, ed. C. H. Talbert and trans. Ralph S. Fraser (Philadelphia: Fortress; London: SCM, 1971). The controversy is widely, though wrongly, held to mark the start of the quest of the historical Jesus. For further discussion see Colin Brown, *Jesus in European Protestant Thought, 1778–1860*, Studies in Historical Theology, no. 1 (Durham, N.C.: Labyrinth, 1985), pp. 1–55, esp. pp. 19ff.

1. God in History

[1] Cited from Kant's article "Beantwortung der Frage: Was ist Aufklärung?" *Berlinische Monatsschrift*, ser. 4, no. 12 (1784): 481–94; trans. Lewis White Beck in his edition of Kant's *Foundations of the Metaphysics of Morals and What is Enlightenment?* (Indianapolis and New York: Bobbs-Merrill, 1959), p. 85. See also Colin Brown, *Jesus in European Protestant Thought, 1778–1860*, pp. 58ff.

[2] See, e.g., Richard H. Popkin, *The History of Skepticism from Erasmus to Spinoza* (Berkeley, Los Angeles, London: University of California Press, 1979).

[3] *Critique of Pure Reason*, trans. Norman Kemp Smith, 2d ed. (1787; reprint, London: Macmillan, 1973), pp. 564ff.

[4] Cf. Ludwig Wittgenstein, *Tractatus Logico-Philosophus* (1921), 6.53–54. Trans. D. F. Pears and B. F. McGuinness (New York: Humanities; London: Routledge & Kegan Paul, 1961), p. 151.

[5] See the interesting discussion of Martin E. Marty, "The Difference in Being a Christian and the Difference it Makes—for History," in C. T. McIntire and Ronald A. Wells, eds., *History and Historical Understanding* (Grand Rapids: Eerdmans, 1984), pp. 41–54.

[6] For a modern restatement of this view see Norman L. Geisler, *Miracles and Modern Thought* (Grand Rapids: Zondervan, 1982). For a review of this and other contemporary discussions see Colin Brown, *Miracles and the Critical Mind*, (Grand Rapids: Eerdmans, 1984), pp. 197–238.

[7] Calvin, *Institutes of the Christian Religion* (1559), Prefatory Address; 1.8.5–7; 1.13.13; cf. Brown, *Miracles*, pp. 15–18.

[8] John Locke, *The Reasonableness of Christianity with A Discourse of Miracles*, ed. Ian T. Ramsey (London: A. & C. Black), p. 81.

[9] *The Reasonableness of Christianity with a Discourse of Miracles*, p. 82. For discussion see Brown, *Miracles*, pp. 41–46.

[10] *Tractatus Theologico-Politicus* (1670), ch. 6. Spinoza's objections were based on his pantheistic view of God and the world. However, he expressed them in language that combined the science of his day with Calvinistic theology. For discussion see Brown, *Miracles*, pp. 30–34.

[11] Trans. R. H. M. Elwes, reprint (New York: Dover, 1951), p. 83.

[12] See Brown, *Miracles*, pp. 47–58; R. M. Burns, *The Great Debate on Miracles: From Joseph Glanvill to David Hume* (Lewisburg: Bucknell University Press; London and Toronto: Associated University Presses, 1981).

[13] Middleton's *Free Inquiry into the Miraculous Powers which are Supposed to have Subsisted in the Christian Church* (1748) was a highly influential critique of miracle stories in the postbiblical period. For discussion see Brown, *Miracles*, pp. 64–72.

[14] Text in Hume's *Enquiries Concerning Christian Understanding*, ed. L. A. Selby-Bigge, 3d ed., rev. by P. H. Nidditch (Oxford: Clarendon, 1975), pp. 109–31. For detailed discussion see Brown, *Miracles*, pp. 79–100.

[15] See, e.g., Matthew 12:28, 38–41; 16:1–4; Luke 11:20; John 2:11, 18–19, 23; 3:2; 4:54; 6:2; 7:31; 9:16; 10:41; 11:47; 12:18, 37; 20:30; Acts 2:22; Hebrews 2:4. See the discussion of signs in Colin Brown, *That You May Believe: Miracles and Faith—Then and Now* (Grand Rapids: Eerdmans, 1985), pp. 74–77, 107–9, 114–17, 148–50, 159–63.

[16] *Essay Concerning Human Understanding* (1690), 4.17.23; reprint, ed. L. A. Selby-Bigge (Oxford: Oxford University Press, 1902), p. 354. For a modern restatement of this view see R. J. Berry, "What to Believe about Miracles," *Nature* 322 (1986): 321–22.

[17] R. F. Holland, "The Miraculous," *American Philosophical Quarterly* 2 (1965): 43–51; reprinted in D. Z. Phillips., ed., *Religion and Understanding* (Oxford: Blackwell, 1967), pp. 155–70. See also Richard Swinburne, *The Concept of Miracle* (London: Macmillan, 1970), pp. 4ff. For H. H. Farmer it is the revelatory aspect

of miracles in answering prayer for succor at a critical stage in personal destiny that constitutes the essence of the miraculous. It is wrong, he argues, to start by discussing it in relation to natural law (*The World and God*, 2d ed. [London: Nisbet, 1935], pp. 107–27). Whereas Farmer gives the impression of trying to avoid a clash between science and religion, M. Polanyi holds the two apart. "It is illogical to attempt the proof of the supernatural aspects by natural tests, for these can only establish the natural aspects of an event and can never represent it as supernatural" (*Personal Knowledge: Toward a Post-Critical Philosophy* [London: Routledge & Kegan Paul, 1958], p. 284). For discussions of the views of Holland, Swinburne, Farmer, and other contemporary philosophers see Brown, *Miracles*, pp. 171–95, 219–38.

18 Holland's example in Phillips, *Religion and Understanding*, pp. 155–56.

19 E.g., Mark 1:23ff.; 2:1–12; 3:3ff.; Acts 3:1–10.

20 Exodus 14:21.

21 Phillips, *Religion and Understanding*, p. 163.

22 Ibid., p. 167.

23 Ibid. pp. 163–64; cf. also C. S. Lewis, *Miracles: A Preliminary Discussion*, rev. ed. (London: Collins, Fontana, 1960), p. 17. See also the discussion of E. L. Mascall, *Christian Theology and Natural Science: Some Questions in their Relations* (London: Longmans, 1957), pp. 167–207; Mary Hesse, "Miracles and the Laws of Nature," in C. F. D. Moule, ed., *Miracles: Cambridge Studies in Their Philosophy and History* (London: Mowbray, 1965), pp. 35–42; Ian G. Barbour, *Issues in Science and Religion* (Englewood Cliffs, N.J.: Prentice-Hall, 1966; London: SCM, 1968), pp. 273–316; A. R. Peacocke, *Science and the Christian Experiment* (London: Oxford University Press, 1971), pp. 35–53.

24 1 Corinthians 15:12–22, 49ff.; Colossians 3:1–4; 1 John 3:2.

25 Cf. Alan Richardson, *The Miracle Stories of the Gospels* (London: SCM, 1941), pp. 45–58; Leon Morris, *The Gospel According to John* (Grand Rapids: Eerdmans, 1971), pp. 684–91; M. E. Glasswell, "The Use of Miracles in the Markan Gospel," and G. W. H. Lampe, "Miracles in the Acts of the Apostles," in Moule, *Miracles*, pp. 151–78.

26 *Enquiries Concerning Human Understanding*, 10, no. 90, n. 1, p. 115.

27 Ibid., 10, no. 90, p. 114.

28 Ibid., 10, no. 92, pp. 116–17.

29 Ibid., 10, no. 93, p. 118.

30 Ibid., 10, no. 94, p. 119.

31 Ibid., 10, no. 95–99, pp. 121–30.

32 Ibid., 10, no. 99, pp. 127–29.

33 Ibid., 10, no. 101, pp. 130–31.

34 Ibid., 10, no. 96, p. 124.

35 Ibid., 10, no. 96, p. 125.

36 *The Concept of Miracle*, p. 17.

37 Ibid., pp. 33–37.

38 Ibid., pp. 60–61.

39 Cf., e.g., Matthew 5:43–48; Acts 14:16–17; Romans 13:1–7; 1 Peter 2:13–17; Revelation 22:2.

40 Romans 1:29–33.

41 Acts 14:15.

42 *Enquiries*, 10, no. 81, p. 110.

43 Cf. P. Nowell-Smith, "Miracles," in Antony Flew and Alasdair MacIntyre, eds., *New Essays in Philosophical Theology* (London: SCM, 1955), p. 253.

44 A. McKinnon, " 'Miracle' and 'Paradox,' " *American Philosophical Quarterly* 4 (1967): 301–14; cf. R. Swinburne, *Concept of Miracle*, pp. 19–20, 23–32.

45 See above, nn. 15, 25.

[46] *Concept of Miracle,* p. 65; cf. also Swinburne's more recent discussion, "Arguments from History and Miracles," in *The Concept of God* (Oxford: Clarendon, 1979), pp. 225–43.

[47] *Concept of Miracle,* pp. 68–69.

[48] Alan Richardson, *History: Sacred and Profane,* Bampton Lectures, 1962, (London: SCM, 1964), p. 206.

[49] Ibid., pp. 206–7. On the question of the empty tomb see H. von Campenhausen, "The Events of Easter and the Empty Tomb," in *Tradition and Life in the Church: Essays and Lectures in Church History,* trans. A. V. Littledale (London: A. & C. Black, 1968), pp. 42–89; James Orr, *The Resurrection of Jesus* (London: Hodder & Stoughton, 1908), pp. 113ff.; Walter Künneth, *The Theology of the Resurrection,* trans. James W. Leitch (London: SCM, 1965), p. 97; C. F. D. Moule, ed., *The Significance of the Message of the Resurrection for Faith in Jesus Christ,* Studies in Biblical Theology, 2d ser., no. 8 (London: SCM, 1968), pp. 7ff.; G. E. Ladd, *I Believe in the Resurrection of Jesus* (Grand Rapids: Eerdmans; London: Hodder & Stoughton, 1975), pp. 79–103, 132–53; Murray J. Harris, *Raised Immortal: Resurrection and Immortality in the New Testament* (London: Marshall, Morgan & Scott; Grand Rapids: Eerdmans, 1983), pp. 37–44, 58–71; William Lane Craig, "The Empty Tomb of Jesus," in R. T. France and David Wenham, eds., *Gospel Perspectives,* vol. 2, *Studies of History and Tradition in the Four Gospels* (Sheffield: JSOT, 1981), pp. 173–200.

[50] *History: Sacred and Profane,* p. 209; cf. W. Pannenberg, *Basic Questions in Theology,* trans. George H. Kehm and R. A. Wilson, 3 vols. (London: SCM, 1970), 1:8: "Only the resurrection of Jesus, conceived in the framework of the cultural situation of primitive Christianity, renders intelligible the early history of Christian faith up to the confessions of Jesus' true divinity. If the resurrection of Jesus cannot be considered to be a historical event, then the historical aspect of the primitive Christian message and its different forms, both of which have crystallized into the New Testament, fall hopelessly apart."

[51] G. Bornkamm, *Jesus of Nazareth,* trans. Irene McLuskey and Fraser McLuskey with James M. Robinson (London: Hodder & Stoughton, 1960), p. 180; cf. Richardson, *History: Sacred and Profane,* p. 196. Richardson's approach may be compared with that of Ian T. Ramsey in "The Logical Character of Resurrection Belief," in his book *Christian Empiricism,* ed. Jerry H. Gill (London: Sheldon, 1974), pp. 177–85.

[52] *History: Sacred and Profane,* pp. 196ff.

[53] Ibid., p. 212. To some, this last point might seem to beg the whole question. But Richardson's point remains that the phenomenon of resurrection faith requires explanation and that this in turn invites hypotheses to account for it. The New Testament data themselves provoke the question whether the resurrection belief described in it entails a physical resuscitation of the corpse of Jesus and no more or whether it entails some form of transformation and theological illumination of the significance of Jesus. Some kind of transformation seems to be suggested by the narratives that indicate that disciples who had known Jesus well failed at first to recognize their risen Lord (e.g., Luke 24:16, 31; John 20:14) and by the way in which he came and went. Theological illumination may also be suggested by the Emmaus road narrative and by Paul's statement of belief in 1 Corinthians 15:4. At the same time there was a continuity of identity between the historical Jesus and the risen Christ.

[54] *History: Sacred and Profane,* p. 212.

[55] Cf., e.g., Matthew 28:1–10; Mark 16:6ff.; Luke 24:1–43; John 20:1–29; Acts 9:1–9; 26:12–19; 1 Corinthians 15:3–11; 1 Peter 1:3; and Wolfhart Pannenberg, *The Apostles' Creed in the Light of Today's Questions,* trans. Margaret Kohl (Philadelphia: Westminster; London: SCM, 1972), p. 97.

The same issue arises in the debate between C. F. D. Moule and D. Cupitt, who argues that "seeing the risen Lord becomes more like seeing the conclusion of an argument than like seeing Edward Heath. . . . In the case of a *religious experience of a transcendent* object, the interpretative work precedes the vision, and does not follow it. So I claim that the Easter faith—the theological affirmation of Jesus' exaltation—must be, logically as well as chronologically, prior to the Easter experiences. That is why only a believer could see the risen Lord: or, to put it more exactly, the Christophany-experience focuses and crystallizes the fact that this man now does beyond doubt "see" and believe in the exaltation of Jesus as Christ" (C. F. D. Moule and D. Cupitt, "The Resurrection: A Disagreement," *Theology* 75 [1972]: 514).

Moule replies: "I still find it difficult, if not impossible, to believe that the disciples had, in the Scriptures and the life, teaching and death of Jesus and their own circumstances, all that was necessary to create the Easter-belief. Granted that they were thrown into an ecstasy of astonishment by what Jesus was and did, something more than this is needed (so it seems to me) to lead to the conclusion that Jesus had been not merely a superlatively great prophet, nor simply a man of the Spirit, nor just Messiah (the latter is an almost impossible conclusion, anyway, after the Crucifixion, without something to suggest it), but that he was alive in a unique and hitherto unexemplified way, and *therefore* Son of God (in a far more than Messianic sense), and "Lord," and the climax and coping-stone of God's plan of salvation" (p. 515; cf. Moule, *The Significance of the Message*, pp. 1–11).

56 For an account of Francis Schaeffer's views on Kierkegaard see Ronald W. Ruegsegger, "Francis Schaeffer on Philosophy," in Ronald W. Ruegsegger, ed., *Reflections on Francis Schaeffer* (Grand Rapids: Zondervan), pp. 107–30, see esp. pp. 118–20.

57 An excellent introduction to Kierkegaard's way of thinking is given by C. Stephen Evans in *Kierkegaard's "Fragments" and "Postscript": The Religious Philosophy of Johannes Climacus* (Atlantic Highlands, N.J.: Humanities, 1983). I have given my own appraisal of Kierkegaard's approach in *Jesus in European Protestant Thought, 1778–1860*, pp. 140–59.

58 *Philosophical Fragments; Johannes Climacus. Kierkegaard's Writings*, vol. 7, ed. and trans. Howard V. Hong and Edna H. Hong (Princeton, N.J.: Princeton University Press, 1985), p. 104.

59 The term applies, of course, to the movement associated with Karl Barth in the 1920s and 1930s that stressed the otherness of God and the sole possibility of knowing him in Christ. In this, Barth was consciously indebted to Kierkegaard. Cf. K. Barth, *The Epistle to the Romans* (1921; reprint, Oxford: Oxford University Press, 1933), pp. 10, 99, and passim; Barth, *God, Grace and Gospel* (*Scottish Journal of Theology*, Occasional Papers, no. 8, 1959), pp. 34ff.; Barth, *Fragments Grave and Gay* (London: Fontana, 1971), pp. 102ff.; C. Brown, *Karl Barth and the Christian Message* (London: Tyndale [Inter-Varsity], 1967), pp. 17ff., 44–45.

60 *Christian Discourses*, trans. Walter Lowrie, 2d ed. (New York: Oxford University Press, Galaxy, 1961), p. 368.

61 *Philosophical Fragments*, pp. 22–48.

62 Ibid., p. 47.

63 Ibid., pp. 21–22, 53–54.

64 Cf. the argument of *Philosophical Fragments*, p. 42, which rejects the inferential proofs of the existence of God from nature and providence in favor of a presuppositionalism comparable with that of Francis Schaeffer. "By beginning, then, I have presupposed the ideality, have presupposed that I will succeed in accomplishing it, but what else is that but presupposing that the god exists and actually beginning with trust in him." See also Kierkegaard's

Concluding Unscientific Postscript to the Philosophical Fragments, trans. D. F. Swenson and W. Lowrie (Princeton, N.J.: Princeton University Press, 1941), pp. 485, 501–2.

[65] *Philosophical Fragments*, pp. 52, 221, 294; *Concluding Unscientific Postscript*, pp. 183–84, 188–89, 235, 496.

[66] *Training in Christianity*, trans. Walter Lowrie, reprint (Princeton, N.J.: Princeton University Press, 1972), pp. 128–31; cf. *Philosophical Fragments*, pp. 55–110.

[67] *Søren Kierkegaard's Journals and Papers*, ed. and trans. Howard V. Hong and Edna H. Hong (Bloomington, Ind., and London: Indiana University Press, 1967), vol. 1, no. 327, p. 138.

[68] *Training*, p. 143.

[69] *Philosophical Fragments*, p. 104.

[70] Matthew 16:17; cf. 13:10–17; Mark 4:11–12; Luke 8:9–10; 1 Corinthians 2:8–16; 2 Corinthians 3:14–18.

[71] On the question of skepticism see P. Carnley, "The Poverty of Historical Scepticism," in S. W. Sykes and J. P. Clayton, eds., *Christ, Faith and History: Cambridge Studies in Christology* (Cambridge: Cambridge University Press, 1972), pp. 165–90.

[72] Isaiah 6:1–13.

[73] Matthew 17:1–9; Mark 9:2–10; Luke 9:28–36.

[74] Matthew 28:1–28; Mark 16:1–8; Luke 24:1–53; John 20:1–21:25.

[75] 2 Corinthians 12:2.

[76] Revelation 1:10–20.

[77] Exodus 33:20.

[78] Matthew 5:8.

[79] 1 Corinthians 13:12.

[80] Cf. Gordon Wenham's discussion of the relationship of theology and history in the Old Testament in Colin Brown, ed., *History, Criticism and Faith*, pp. 16ff.; and also the discussion below in ch. 2.

The unhistorical use of the past to interpret the present has come under valid criticism from J. H. Plumb in *The Death of the Past* (Harmondsworth: Pelican, 1973). Nevertheless, Plumb himself is anxious to draw lessons from the past, and even as a historian with strong rationalistic inclinations he permits himself to pass moral judgments on history (p. 113).

"Historians can use history to fulfill many of the social purposes which the old mythical pasts did so well. It can no longer provide sanctions for authority, nor for aristocratic or oligarchical elites, nor for inherent destinies clothed in national guise, but it can still teach wisdom, and it can teach it in a far deeper sense than was possible when wisdom had to be taught through the example of heroes" (pp. 113–14).

It may be noted that Plumb appears to confine human achievement in history and in general to reason and rationalism, though these are somewhat ill defined. His concept of rationalism seems to oscillate between that which he attributes to Gibbon and the Enlightenment on the one hand, and to the valid application of reason wherever it can be found on the other hand. In the latter case reason is hardly a monopoly of any particular school or outlook.

[81] See, e.g., *Escape from Reason* (Downers Grove and London: InterVarsity, 1968); and *He is There and He is Not Silent* (Wheaton: Tyndale; London: Hodder & Stoughton, 1972). For judicious appraisals of Francis Schaeffer's philosophy and apologetics see the articles by Forrest Baird, Gordon R. Lewis, and Ronald W. Ruegsegger in Ruegsegger, *Reflections on Francis Schaeffer*, pp. 45–130.

[82] On Richardson's approach to history see esp. his *The Miracle Stories of the Gospels* (London: SCM, 1941); *Christian Apologetics* (London: SCM, 1947), pp. 89–109; *The Bible in the Age of Science* (London: SCM, 1961), pp. 54–76; *An*

Introduction to the Theology of the New Testament (London: SCM, 1958), pp. 1–15; *History: Sacred and Profane* (London: SCM, 1964); and J. J. Navone, *History and Faith in the Thought of Alan Richardson* (London: SCM, 1966).

83 *Introduction to the Theology of the New Testament*, p. 9; cf. *Christian Apologetics*, pp. 104–9. Cf. the "perspectivism" of Karl Heussi in *Die Krisis des Historismus* (Tübingen: Mohr [Siebeck], 1932) and of Bernard Lonergan in *Method in Theology* (London: Darton, Longman & Todd, 1972), pp. 214–20.

84 *Introduction to the Theology of the New Testament*, p. 13.

85 Scientific theories are about recurrent phenomena, not isolated events. The historian cannot test his theories by controlled experiment. Nor has he direct access to his subject matter. On the other hand, his work is open to repeated public testing by himself or anyone else who has the necessary knowledge and skills.

Richardson's account may be compared with the following description by the philosopher of science C. G. Hempel:

"Scientific hypotheses and theories are not *derived* from observed facts, but *invented* in order to account for them. They constitute guesses at the connections that might obtain between the phenomena under study, at uniformities and patterns that might underlie the occurrence. 'Happy guesses' of this kind require great ingenuity, especially if they involve a radical departure from current modes of scientific thinking, as did, for example, the theory of relativity and the quantum theory. The inventive effort required in scientific research will benefit from a thorough familiarity with current knowledge in the field. A complete novice will hardly make an important scientific discovery, for the ideas that may occur to him are likely to duplicate what has been tried before or to run afoul of well-established facts or theories of which he is not aware" (*Philosophy of Natural Science* [Englewood Cliffs, N.J.: Prentice-Hall, 1966], p. 15).

86 *Introduction to the Theology of the New Testament*, p. 12.

87 On the notion of "paradigm shifts" in science see Thomas S. Kuhn, *The Structure of Scientific Revolutions*, 2d ed. (Chicago: University of Chicago Press, 1970). For a review of Kuhn's position see W. H. Newton Smith, *The Rationality of Science* (Boston, London, and Henley: Routledge & Kegan Paul, 1981), pp. 102–24 and passim.

2. Rules, Principles, and Explanations

1 *The Idea of History* (London: Oxford University Press, 1946; reprinted with alterations, 1961), p. 252.

2 *The Historian and the Believer: The Morality of Historical Knowledge and Christian Belief* (New York: Macmillan, 1966; London: SCM, 1967), p. 45. Cf. P. Gardiner, *The Nature of Historical Explanation* (London: Oxford University Press, 1961), pp. 28ff.; P. Gardiner, ed., *Theories of History* (Glencoe, Ill.: Free Press, 1959), pp. 344–475; W. H. Dray, *Philosophy of History* (Englewood Cliffs, N.J.: Prentice-Hall, 1964), pp. 4ff.; W. H. Dray, ed., *Philosophical Analysis and History* (Englewood Cliffs, N.J.: Prentice-Hall, 1966); A. C. Danto, *Analytical Philosophy of History* (London: Cambridge University Press, 1965); W. H. Walsh, *An Introduction to the Philosophy of History* (London: Hutchinson, 1951), pp. 30–71; M. White, *Foundations of Historical Knowledge* (New York: Harper & Row, 1965); J. H. Hexter, *Doing History* (Bloomington, Ind.: Indiana University Press; London: Allen & Unwin, 1971).

The debate may be illustrated by J. H. Hexter's rebuttal of C. G. Hempel's attempt to assimilate history to the procedures of natural science. In "The Function of General Laws in History" (*Journal of Philosophy* 39 [1943]: 35–48;

reprinted in Gardiner, *Theories of History*, pp. 344–55), Hempel argued that historical research should be conducted by reference to general laws analogous to those of the natural sciences. This involves linking events with general laws. It is precisely this which distinguishes genuine explanations from false. "Historical explanation . . . aims at showing that the event in question was not 'a matter of chance,' but was to be expected in view of certain antecedent or simultaneous conditions. The expectation referred to is not prophecy or divination, but rational scientific anticipation which rests on the assumption of general laws" (*Theories of History*, pp. 348–49).

Writing as a practicing historian, Hexter also claims that history is "a rule-bound discipline," but he contends that the process of writing history is not something secondary and incidental but is essential to conveying the inward character of the past as it really was. Moreover, the vocabulary and syntax that constitute the appropriate response of the historian to his data are not identifiable with those of the scientist. "The historian's goal in response to his data is to render the best account he can of the past as it really was" (*Doing History*, p. 68). To do this he must employ a language which sacrifices generality, precision, and control to evocative force and scope. It implies that the language of history contains embedded in itself assumptions about the nature of knowing, understanding, meaning, and truth which are not completely congruent with those of the sciences, at least in so far as the philosophy of science has identified them.

A similar view is argued by Ian T. Ramsey in his inaugural lecture at Oxford, "Miracles: An Exercise in Logical Mapwork" (reprinted in *The Miracles and the Resurrection: Some Recent Studies* by I. T. Ramsey, G. H. Boobyer, F. N. Davey, M. C. Perry, and Henry J. Cadbury [London: SPCK, 1964], pp. 1–30). Ramsey suggests that scientists and historians are engaged in two types of map making that are different but interrelated. Among other things, the scientist deals with what is general and repeatable, whereas the historian deals with the unique and the personal.

[3] *Historian and Believer*, p. 54. Cf. Swinburne's discussion of principles for weighing conflicting evidence:

"The most basic principle is to accept as many pieces of evidence as possible. If one witness says one thing, and five witnesses say a different thing, then, in the absence of further evidence (e.g., about their unreliability) take the testimony of the latter. If one method of dating an artifact gives one result, and five methods give a different result, then, in the absence of further information accept the latter result. The first subsidiary principle is—apart from any empirical evidence about their relative reliability—that evidence of different kinds ought to be given different weights. How this is to be done can only be illustrated by examples. Thus one's own apparent memory ought as such to count for more than the testimony of another witness (unless and until evidence of its relative unreliability is forthcoming). . . . If the testimony of Jones conflicts with the testimony of Smith, then we must investigate not the worth of testimony in general, but the worth of Jones' testimony and of Smith's testimony. We do this by seeing if, on all other occasions when we can ascertain what happened, Jones or Smith correctly described what happened. In so far as each did, his testimony is reliable. . . . The third subsidiary principle is not to reject coincident evidence (unless the evidence of its falsity is extremely strong) unless an explanation can be given of the coincidence; and the better substantiated is that explanation, the more justified the rejection of the coincident evidence" (*The Concept of Miracle* [London: Macmillan, 1970], pp. 37–39).

[4] *Historian and Believer*, pp. 51ff. It is interesting to note that Oscar Cullmann uses a similar argument as proof of Jesus' messianic consciousness against the

contention of the Bultmann school that Jesus did not think of himself as the messianic Son of Man, or figure in his own preaching. "The historical fact that Jesus was condemned by the Romans (of course in complete misunderstanding of his 'self-consciousness') as a Zealot, as a pretender to the throne (cf. the 'titulus' on top of the cross), seems to me to be almost irrefutable proof that Jesus in some way made himself the subject of his preaching on the Kingdom of God soon to come" (*Salvation in History*, trans. Sidney G. Sowers et al. [London: SCM; New York: Harper & Row, 1967], p. 109; cf. Cullmann, *The State in the New Testament* [New York: Scribner, 1956; London: SCM, 1957], pp. 8–49).

I have taken Harvey's analysis of the reasons for the crucifixion of Jesus not as a complete and final statement of the reasons but as a good example of *the dynamics of historical thinking*. For more information on the practice of crucifixion see Martin Hengel, *Crucifixion: In the Ancient World and the Folly of the Message of the Cross*, trans. John Bowden (Philadelphia: Fortress; London: SCM, 1977). For discussions of the political background see Ernst Bammel and C. F. D. Moule, eds., *Jesus and the Politics of His Day* (Cambridge: Cambridge University Press, 1984).

As I have argued in *Miracles and the Critical Mind, That You May Believe*, and the "Note on the Gospel Miracles" at the end of the present book, I believe that a significant but neglected factor in the Jewish opposition to Jesus was the conviction that Jesus was a wonder-working prophet of the kind described in Deuteronomy 13, who was leading the people astray. Early on the authorities came to the conclusion that Jesus should be purged from the midst of the people in accordance with the teaching of Deuteronomy 13. An account of the trial of Jesus that takes these factors into account is August Strobel, *Die Stunde der Wahrheit. Untersuchungen zum Strafverfahren gegen Jesu, Wissenschaftliche Untersuchungen zum Neuen Testament*, vol. 21 (Tübingen: Mohr [Siebeck], 1980). This view would have significant bearing on the reasons for the crucifixion.

[5] *Historian and Believer*, pp. 54–59.

[6] The application of a new methodology to traditional sources is illustrated by the work of a colleague of mine at Fuller Theological Seminary, Dr. James E. Bradley. Dr. Bradley has made a study of popular political behavior and religion in England during the American Revolution. Dr. Bradley's book *Popular Politics and the American Revolution* (Macon, Ga.: Mercer University Press, 1986) examines petitions to the king protesting the government's policy of coercion in the colonies. These petitions were signed by hundreds of concerned citizens; the names of these people were transcribed, alphabetized, and linked to the names found in Presbyterian, Congregational, and Baptist chapel registers. This method of linking two otherwise unrelated lists of names, known as nominal record linkage, enabled Dr. Bradley to draw conclusions concerning the measure of support for conciliation with the colonies, which in turn challenge some of the current assumptions about this period of history.

[7] "History" in *Avenues of History* (London: Hamish Hamilton, 1952), cited from Fritz Stern, ed., *The Varieties of History: From Voltaire to the Present*, 2d ed. (New York and London: Macmillan, 1970), p. 375. Cf. also M. Polanyi, *Personal Knowledge: Towards a Post-Critical Philosophy* (London: Routledge & Kegan Paul; Chicago: University of Chicago Press, 1958), p. 321.

[8] *Historian and Believer*, p. 61.

[9] Ibid.

[10] *History, Archaeology and Christian Humanism* (New York: McGraw-Hill, 1964), p. 26.

[11] Cf. E. H. Carr, *What is History?* reprint (Hardmondsworth: Pelican, 1964), pp. 87–108; Alan Richardson, *History: Sacred and Profane*, Bampton Lectures, 1962 (London: SCM, 1964), pp. 97ff., 170.

[12] Carr, *What Is History?* pp. 7–30; Richardson, *History: Sacred and Profane*, pp. 154–93, 190–94; R. G. Collingwood, *Idea of History*, pp. 249–82; Ian T. Ramsey, "Facts and Disclosures," in his *Christian Empiricism*, ed. Jerry H. Gill (London: Sheldon, 1974), pp. 159–76.

[13] In a valid deduction the conclusion is related to the premises in such a way that, if the premises are true, the conclusion must also be true. In induction inferences are drawn from a number of cases that point to a general conclusion. C. G. Hempel strongly repudiates the idea that the natural sciences are based on pure induction, involving observation of all facts without prior selection or guesses as to their relative importance, followed by analysis and classification, inductive derivation of generalizations from them and further testing of these generalizations (*Philosophy of Natural Science* [Englewood Cliffs, N.J.: Prentice-Hall, 1966], pp. 10–18). For him there are no general rules of induction. "The transition from data to theory requires creative imagination. Scientific hypotheses and theories are not *derived* from observed facts, but *invented* in order to account for them" (p. 15).

This may be compared with E. H. Carr's account of the historian's procedure.

"The historian starts with a provisional selection of facts, and a provisional interpretation in the light of which that selection has been made—by others as well as by himself. As he works, both the interpretation and the selection and ordering of facts undergo subtle and perhaps unconscious changes, through the reciprocal action of the one on the other. And this reciprocal action also involves reciprocity between the present and past, since the historian is part of the present and the facts belong to the past. The historian and the facts are necessary to one another. The historian without his facts is rootless and futile; the facts without their historian are dead and meaningless. My first answer therefore to the question 'What is history?' is that it is a continuous process of interaction between the historian and his facts, an unending dialogue between the present and the past" (*What Is History?* pp. 29–30).

In the natural sciences it is not enough to produce a hypothesis which might explain certain phenomena but which is at variance with accepted thought (cf. Hempel, *Natural Science*, p. 15; and see above, ch. 1, n. 85).

[14] R. G. Collingwood has drawn attention to the way in which an established view may be used to test the veracity of a piece of testimony in cases where there is no contradictory testimony.

"The web of imaginative construction is something far more solid and powerful than we have hitherto realized. So far from relying for its validity upon the support of given facts, it actually serves as the touchstone by which we decide whether alleged facts are genuine. Suetonius tells me that Nero at one time intended to evacuate Britain. I reject his statement, not because any better authority flatly contradicts it, for of course none does; but because my reconstruction of Nero's policy based on Tacitus will not allow me to think that Suetonius is right. And if I am told that this is merely to say I prefer Tacitus to Suetonius, I confess that I do: but I do so just because I find myself able to incorporate what Tacitus tells me into a coherent and continuous picture of my own, and cannot do this for Suetonius" (*Idea of History*, p. 244).

Recognition of this process, which often operates for good or ill at a subconscious level, is important. It has a positive value, but it is also open to abuse if one clings to a theory regardless of empirical data. The viability of a theory depends on its ability to account for both instances and counterinstances. When the latter are sufficiently strong there must come a point where the theory must be modified or abandoned.

[15] See also C. L. Becker in P. L. Snyder, ed., *Detachment and the Writing of History: Essays and Letters of Carl L. Becker* (Ithaca, N.Y., and London: Cornell

University Press), pp. 34–35; Bernard Lonergan, *Method in Theology* (London: Darton, Longman and Todd, 1972), pp. 203–14; R. G. Collingwood, *The Idea of History*, pp. 249–82.

[16]G. E. Ladd writes in *The New Testament and Criticism* (Grand Rapids: Eerdmans, 1967; London: Hodder & Stoughton, 1970):

"An evangelical criticism as well as rationalistic criticism must often be satisfied with hypotheses, probabilities, possibilities, rather than in dogmatic certainties, as distasteful as this may be to the uncritical mind which insists on 'thus saith the Lord' in every detail of Bible study. Such questions as the original ending of Mark, the precise meaning of *dokimon*, . . . the authorship of the first Gospel, the *Sitz im Leben* of the Gospel of John, the nature of the problem Paul faced in the church in Corinth (whether Jewish or Gnostic), the degree to which God in redemptive history has made use of elements from the Jewish and Hellenistic environments—all these do not constitute the content of revealed truth but are aspects of the historical media through which revelation has been given" (p. 216).

[17]For surveys see, e.g., Henning Graf Reventlow, *Problems of Old Testament Theology in the Twentieth Century*, trans. John Bowden (Philadelphia: Fortress; London, SCM, 1985); *Problems of Biblical Theology in the Twentieth Century*, trans. John Bowden (Philadelphia: Fortress; London: SCM, 1986); G. E. Ladd, *The New Testament and Criticism*; Robert Davidson and A. R. C. Leaney, *The Pelican Guide to Modern Theology*, vol. 3, *Biblical Criticism* (Harmondsworth: Pelican Books, 1970); I. Howard Marshall, ed., *New Testament Interpretation: Essays on Principles and Methods* (Grand Rapids: Eerdmans; Exeter: Paternoster, 1977).

[18]Following Rudolf Bultmann's *The History of the Synoptic Tradition*, trans. John Marsh (1921; reprint, Oxford: Blackwell, 1963), a number of scholars took the view that if a saying attributed in the Gospels to Jesus fit the situation of the postresurrection church, it should be treated as a creation of the church. If a saying or item of teaching fit the world of Judaism, it too could not be treated as authentic on the grounds that Jesus' teaching must be unique and distinctive. Moreover, if the teaching had a Greek rather than Aramaic ring to it, it should be seen as belonging to the Greek world rather than to the world of Jesus. However, these criteria now appear to many scholars to be arbitrary and unworkable. There is no a priori reason why some of Jesus' teaching at least could not apply both to his own lifetime and to a later situation. Likewise, it is arbitrary to insist that Jesus' piety and outlook could have nothing in common with other Jewish teachers, who in any case were also indebted to the Scriptures. It is also arbitrary to assume that the teaching of Jesus could not have been accurately translated into Greek and that only poor translations of his words merit consideration as authentic. For further discussion see Colin Brown, "Bultmann Revisited," *The Churchman* 88 (1974): 167–87, esp. pp. 169–71, 176–81; R. T. France, "The Authenticity of the Sayings of Jesus," in Brown, *History, Criticism and Faith*, pp. 101–43, esp. pp. 110–14; R. T. France and David Wenham, eds., *Gospel Perspectives*, vol. 1, *Studies of History and Tradition in the Four Gospels* (Sheffield: JSOT, 1980), esp. Robert H. Stein, "The 'Criteria' for Authenticity," pp. 225–63, though the other contributions here are also relevant; Rainer Riesner, *Jesus als Lehrer. Eine Untersuchung zum Ursprung der Evangelien-Uberlieferung, Wissenschaftliche Untersuchungen zum Neuen Testament*, 2. Reihe 7 (Tübingen: Mohr [Siebeck], 1981).

[19]On the background to this debate see J. M. Robinson and J. B. Cobb, eds., *The New Hermeneutic: Discussions among American and Continental Theologians* (New York: Harper & Row, 1964); C. E. Braaten, *History and Hermeneutics, New Directions in Theology Today*, vol. 2 (Philadelphia: Westminster, 1966; London: Lutterworth, 1968); R. W. Funk, ed., *History and Hermeneutic, Journal for Theology and the Church*, vol. 4 (New York: Harper & Row, 1967); Anthony C. Thiselton,

The Two Horizons: New Testament Hermeneutic and Philosophical Description (Grand Rapids: Eerdmans; Exeter: Paternoster, 1980); Donald K. McKim, ed., *A Guide to Contemporary Hermeneutics* (Grand Rapids: Eerdmans, 1986).

[20] See Rudolf Bultmann, "New Testament and Mythology," in H. W. Bartsch, ed., *Kerygma and Myth: A Theological Debate*, 1-vol. ed., trans. Reginald H. Fuller (London: SPCK, 1972), pp. 1–44; Bultmann, *Jesus Christ and Mythology*, trans. Paul Schubert et al. (New York: Scribner; London: SCM, 1958); Bultmann, *History and Eschatology: The Presence of Eternity*, The Gifford Lectures 1955 (Edinburgh: Edinburgh University Press; New York: Harper & Row, 1957); Bultmann, *New Testament and Mythology and Other Basic Writings*, selected, ed., and trans. Schubert M. Ogden (Philadelphia: Fortress, 1984); Walter Schmithals, *An Introduction to the Theology of Rudolf Bultmann*, trans. John Bowden (Minneapolis: Augsburg; London: SCM, 1968); Charles W. Kegley, ed., *The Theology of Rudolf Bultmann* (New York: Harper & Row; London: SCM, 1966).

[21] In addition to the works mentioned in nn. 18 and 20 see also John Macquarrie, *An Existentialist Theology: A Comparison of Heidegger and Bultmann* (London: SCM, 1955); L. Malevez, *The Christian Message and Myth: The Theology of Rudolf Bultmann*, trans. Olive Wyon (London: SCM, 1958); André Malet, *The Thought of Rudolf Bultmann*, trans. Richard Strachan with preface by Rudolf Bultmann (Shannon, Ire.: Irish University Press, 1969); Roger A. Johnson, *The Origins of Demythologizing: Philosophy and Historiography in the Theology of Rudolf Bultmann*, Studies in the History of Religions (Supplements to *Numen*), no. 28 (Leiden: Brill, 1974); F. F. Bruce, "Myth and History," in Colin Brown, ed., *The New International Dictionary of New Testament Theology*, 3 vols. with index (Grand Rapids: Zondervan; Exeter: Paternoster, 1976), 2:643–47; Wolfhart Pannenberg, "The Later Dimensions of Myth in Biblical and Christian Tradition" in *Basic Questions in Theology*, 3 vols. (London: SCM, 1973), 3:1–79 (in the United States this book has the title *The Idea of God and Human Freedom*[Philadelphia: Westminster]); A. C. Thiselton, *The Two Horizons*, pp. 205–92, esp. pp. 252–75; G. B. Caird, *The Language and Imagery of the Bible* (Philadelphia: Westminster, 1980), pp. 201–71, esp. pp. 219–42.

I agree with Earl R. MacCormac in seeing myth as the false attribution of reality to a suggestive metaphor and in seeing that myth has played a formative part not only in religion and history but also in scientific thought (see Earl R. MacCormac, *Metaphor and Myth in Science and Religion* [Durham, N.C.: Duke University Press, 1976]). For this reason it is important to distinguish mythological language from the language of metaphor and symbolism and to be able to identify usage.

[22] "Ueber historische und dogmatische Methode in der Theologie," reprinted in Ernst Troeltsch, *Gesammelte Schriften*, vol. 2, *Zur religiösen Lage, Religionsphilosophie und Ethik*, Neudruck der 2. Auflage 1922 (Aalen: Scientia Verlag, 1962), pp. 729–53; cf. also Troeltsch's article "Historiography," in J. Hastings, ed., *Encyclopaedia of Religion and Ethics*, 13 vols. (Edinburgh: T. & T. Clark, 1914), 4:716–23; and E. Troeltsch, *The Absoluteness of Christianity and the History of Religions*, trans. David Reid (London: SCM, 1972).

[23] Author's translation from *Gesammelte Schriften*, 2:732. This translation also appears in my book *Miracles and the Critical Mind*, pp. 128–29, in conjunction with a discussion of the attitudes of Troeltsch, Bousset, and the History-of-Religions School to the miraculous.

[24] Cited from Pannenberg's essay "Redemptive Event and History," *Basic Questions*, 1:46. Cf. also the discussions of Carl E. Braaten, *History and Hermeneutics*, pp. 98–101; Jürgen Moltmann, *Theology of Hope: On the Ground and Implications of a Christian Eschatology*, trans. James W. Leitch (London: SCM; New York: Harper & Row, 1967), pp. 172–82.

25 *Basic Questions*, 1:49; cf. also Pannenberg's discussion of the resurrection of Jesus as a historical problem in *Jesus—God and Man*, trans. Lewis L. Wilkins and Duane E. Priebe (London: SCM; Philadelphia: Westminster, 1968), pp. 88–106.

26 Cited from F. Stern, ed., *Varieties of History*, p. 378.

27 T. F. Torrance writes in *Theological Science* (London: Oxford University Press, 1969):

"Our primary task, epistemologically, is to focus our attention on the area where God is actually known, and to seek to understand that knowledge in its concrete happening, out of its own proper ground, and in its own proper reference to objective reality. Scientific procedure will not allow us to go beyond the boundary set by the object, for that would presume that by the inherent powers of our 'autonomous reason' we can gain mastery over it. We have to act within the limits imposed by nature of the object, and avoid self-willed and undisciplined speculative thinking. It would be uncontrolled and unscientific procedure to run ahead of the object and prescribe just how it shall or can be known before we actually know it, or to withdraw ourselves from actual knowing and then in detachment from the object lay down the conditions upon which valid knowledge is possible. . . . Hence even though we know God in the givenness of faith, it is not faith that is the given subject-matter of theology but the God in whom we have faith" (pp. 25–26, 28).

28 *Space, Time and Incarnation* (London: Oxford University Press, 1969), p. 13.

29 Ibid., p. 18.

30 Ibid., pp. 20–21.

31 This process is not, of course, confined to the biblical writers. We do this in everyday life. The plain, old-fashioned name for it is wisdom. The obvious danger is to read false parallels into situations (see Namier's strictures above, p. 47). Nevertheless, dangers and misapplication do not invalidate proper use.

32 Cf., e.g., Psalms 105–107.

33 1 Peter 1:1; 2:9, 11.

34 The question of the use of the Old Testament in the New Testament has received considerable attention in recent years. Among the numerous important studies are the following: E. Earle Ellis, *Paul's Use of the Old Testament* (Edinburgh: Oliver & Boyd, 1957); Ellis, *Prophecy and Hermeneutic in Early Christianity: New Testament Essays, Wissenschaftliche Untersuchungen zum Neuen Testament*, no. 18 (Tübingen: Mohr [Siebeck], 1978); Krister Stendahl, *The School of St. Matthew and its Use of the Old Testament, Acta Seminarii Neotestamentici Upsaliensis*, no. 20, 2d ed. (Lund: Gleerup, 1967); Barnabas Lindars, *New Testament Apologetic: The Doctrinal Significance of the Old Testament Quotations* (London: SCM, 1961); Robert H. Gundry, *The Use of the Old Testament in St. Matthew's Gospel with Special Reference to the Messianic Hope, Supplements to Novum Testamentum*, no. 18 (Leiden: Brill, 1967); R. T. France, *Jesus and the Old Testament: His Application of Old Testament Passages to Himself and His Mission* (London: Tyndale, 1971); R. N. Longenecker, "Can We Reproduce the Exegesis of the New Testament?" *Tyndale Bulletin* 21 (1970): 3–38; *Biblical Exegesis in the Apostolic Period* (Grand Rapids: Eerdmans, 1975); F. F. Bruce, *This is That: The New Testament Development of Some Old Testament Themes* (Exeter: Paternoster; Grand Rapids: Eerdmans, 1968); Bruce, *The Time is Fulfilled: Five Aspects of Fulfillment of the Old Testament in the New Testament* (Grand Rapids: Eerdmans; Exeter: Paternoster, 1978); Dwight Moody Smith, Jr., "The Use of the Old Testament in the New," in J. M. Efird, ed., *The Use of the Old Testament in the New and Other Essays* (Durham, N.C.: Duke University Press, 1972), pp. 3–65; Anthony Tyrrell Hanson, *Studies in Paul's Technique and Theology* (London: SPCK, 1974); Hanson, *The Living Utterances of God: The New Testament Exegesis of the Old* (London: Darton, Longman and Todd, 1983); Bruce D. Chilton, *A*

Galilean Rabbi and His Bible: Jesus' Use of the Interpreted Scripture of His Time, Good News Studies, no. 8 (Wilmington, Del.: Glazier, 1984).

[35] *Basic Questions*, 1:53.

3. What Does the Historian Achieve?

[1] *Geschichte der romanischen und germanischen Völker, 1494–1535* (Berlin: Reimer, 1824), preface (*Sämtliche Werke*, Leipzig, XXXIII, p. vii). A translation of the preface is given in Fritz Stern, ed., *The Varieties of History: From Voltaire to the Present*, 2d ed. (New York and London: Macmillan, 1970), pp. 55–58.

[2] The notion that history is a matter of presenting all the facts and letting them speak for themselves was denounced as "preposterous" by C. L. Becker, "first, because it is impossible to present all the facts; and second, because even if you could present all the facts the miserable things wouldn't say anything, would just say nothing at all" (*Detachment and the Writing of History: Essays and Letters of Carl L. Becker* [Ithaca, N.Y., and London: Cornell University Press, 1958], p. 54; cf. Bernard Lonergan, *Method in Theology* [London: Darton, Longman & Todd, 1972], p. 203).

[3] (London: Oxford University Press, 1954), p. 53.

[4] *History and Human Relations* (London: Collins, 1951), p. 103. Cf. E. Nagel: "It is an obvious blunder to suppose that only a fat cowherd can drive fat kine. It is an equally crude error to maintain that one cannot inquire into the conditions and consequences of values and evaluations without necessarily engaging in moral or aesthetic value judgments" ("The Logic of Historical Analysis," in H. Meyerhoff, ed., *The Philosophy of History in our Time* [Garden City: Doubleday, 1959], p. 161).

[5] *Philosophy of History* (Englewood Cliffs, N.J.: Prentice-Hall, 1964), p. 26. Dray notes, however, the thesis of H. L. A. Hart that "action" is an "ascriptive" rather than a purely "descriptive" concept, in "The Ascription of Responsibility and Rights," in Antony Flew, ed., *Logic and Language*, First Series. (Oxford: Blackwell, 1951), pp. 145–66; cf. G. Pitcher's comments, "Hart on Action and Responsibility," *Philosophical Review* 69 (1960): 226–35.

[6] Reprinted in Stern, *Varieties of History*, pp. 315–28.

[7] Ibid., p. 323.

[8] Ibid., pp. 323–24.

[9] Ibid., p. 324.

[10] Ibid., p. 325.

[11] Cited from Karl Löwith's account of Burckhardt in *Meaning in History: The Theological Implications of the Philosophy of History* (Chicago: University of Chicago Press, 1949), p. 20. See also W. H. Dray's discussion (*Philosophy of History*, p. 28). In similar vein is Jacques Barzun's contention that the expression "Exist in history" could be translated by "are memorable" (Barzun's "Cultural History: A Synthesis" reprinted in Stern, *Varieties of History*, pp. 387–402, see esp. p. 397.)

[12] Cf. E. H. Carr, *What is History?* reprint (Hardmondsworth: Pelican, 1964), p. 29; R. G. Collingwood, *The Idea of History* (London: Oxford University Press, 1946; reprinted with alterations, 1961), pp. 257–61; J. H. Hexter, "The Historian and his Day," reprinted in Hexter's *Reappraisals in History: New Views on History and Society in Early Modern Europe* (London: Longmans, Green & Co., 1961; New York: Harper & Row, 1963), pp. 1–13.

[13] *Annals*, 15.44.4.

[14] Cf. Karl Heussi, *Die Krisis des Historismus* (Tübingen: Mohr, 1932); Lonergan, *Method in Theology*, pp. 214–20; D. M. Baillie, *God Was in Christ: An Essay on Incarnation and Atonement* (London: Faber & Faber, 1956), p. 109.

[15]See the discussion of historical narrative in J. H. Hexter, "The Rhetoric of History," in D. L. Sills, ed., *The International Encyclopedia of Social Sciences* (New York: Macmillan, 1968), 6:368–94; reprinted in J. H. Hexter, *Doing History* (Bloomington, Ind., and London: Indiana University Press, 1971), pp. 15–76.

[16]Cited from Stern, *Varieties of History*, pp. 378–79.

[17]*M. Manilii Astronomicon Liber Primus*, 2d ed. (Cambridge: Cambridge University Press, 1937), p. 87.

[18]Hebrew uses the device of inserting *lēʾmōr* ("saying"), and Greek the word *hoti* ("that"), before giving the contents of an utterance. This was the nearest equivalent to inverted commas that the Greek language had. On New Testament usage see Robert W. Funk, *A Greek Grammar of the New Testament and Other Early Christian Literature* (Cambridge: Cambridge University Press; Chicago: Chicago University Press, 1961), no. 470, pp. 246–47. While the use of such devices indicates the writer's intention of reporting the content of what was said, it cannot be taken to imply that the writer was consciously adopting the same conventions of verbatim quotation that quotation marks imply today.

[19]In recent years the question of what exactly is a gospel has received much attention. For literature on the subject and views see F. F. Bruce, "When is a Gospel not a Gospel?" (*Bulletin of the John Rylands Library* 45 [1963]: 319–39; Robert H. Gundry, "Recent Investigations into the Literary Genre 'Gospel,'" in Richard N. Longenecker and Merrill C. Tenney, eds., *New Dimensions in New Testament Study* (Grand Rapids: Zondervan, 1974), pp. 97–114; C. H. Talbert, *What is a Gospel? The Genre of the Canonical Gospels* (Philadelphia: Fortress, 1977); D. E. Aune, "The Problem of the Genre of the Gospels: A Critique of C. H. Talbert's *What is a Gospel?*" in R. T. France and David Wenham, eds., *Gospel Perspectives*, no. 2. *Studies of History and Tradition in the Four Gospels* (Sheffield: JSOT, 1981), pp. 9–60.

[20]See, e.g., Max Black, *Models and Metaphors: Studies in Language and Philosophy* (Ithaca, N.Y.: Cornell University Press, 1962), esp. pp. 219–43; R. B. Braithwaite, *Scientific Explanation* (Cambridge: Cambridge University Press, 1953); E. L. Mascall, *Christian Theology and Natural Science: Some Questions in their Relations*, Bampton Lectures, 1956 (London: Longmans, Green and Co., 1956), pp. 65–76; Ian T. Ramsey, *Religious Language: An Empirical Placing of Theological Phrases* (London: SCM, 1957), pp. 49–89; Ramsey, *Christian Empiricism*, ed. Jerry H. Gill (London: Sheldon, 1974), pp. 120–58; Ian G. Barbour, *Myths, Models and Paradigms: The Nature of Scientific and Religious Language* (New York: Harper & Row; London: SCM, 1974).

Barbour sees *theoretical models* as "imaginative mental constructs invented to account for observed phenomena. Such a model is usually an imagined mechanism or process, which is postulated by analogy with familiar mechanisms or processes. I will maintain that its chief use is to help one understand the world, not simply to make predictions. But I will also claim that it is not a literal picture of the world. Like a mathematical model, it is a symbolic representation of a physical system, but it differs in its intent to represent the underlying structure of the world. It is used to develop a theory which in some sense explains phenomena. And its origination seems to require a special kind of creative imagination" (*Myths, Models and Paradigms*, p. 30). Barbour's work proceeds to examine the concept of the model and its usefulness in religious discourse.

[21]Cf. M. Bloch: "When all is said and done, a single word, 'Understanding,' is the beacon light of our studies" (*The Historian's Craft*, trans. Peter Putnam [Manchester: Manchester University Press, 1954], p. 143).

[22]*Idea of History*, pp. 282–302.

[23]Trans. from W. Dilthey, "Plan der Fortsetzung zum Aufbau der geschichtlichen Welt in den Geisteswissenschaften," in *Gesammelte Schriften* (Leipzig and Berlin: Teubner, 1927) 7:215. See further the discussion in H. A. Hodges, *The Philosophy of Wilhelm Dilthey* (London: Routledge & Kegan Paul, 1952), pp. 275ff.; and Collingwood, *Idea of History*, pp. 71–76, 314–15.

See also Wolfhart Pannenberg, *Basic Questions in Theology*, trans. George H. Kehm and R. A. Wilson, 3 vols. (London: SCM, 1970), 1:8; Hans-Georg Gadamer, *Truth and Method*, trans. Garrett Barden and John Cumming (New York: Seabury; London: Sheed and Ward, 1975), pp. 267–74, 333–45, 357–66.

The position that Dilthey advocates stands in contrast with that of Bultmann, who concluded his Gifford Lectures by saying:

"The meaning in history always lies in the present, and when the present is conceived as the eschatological present by Christian faith the meaning in history is realized. Man who complains: 'I cannot see meaning in history, and therefore my life, interwoven in history, is meaningless,' is to be admonished: do not look around yourself into universal history, you must look into your own personal history. Always in your present lies the meaning in history, and you cannot see it as a spectator, but only in your responsible decisions. In every moment slumbers the possibility of being the eschatological moment. You must awaken it" (*History and Eschatology: The Presence of Eternity* [Edinburgh: Edinburgh University Press; New York: Harper & Row, 1957], p. 155).

4. How Does History Affect Belief?

[1]On the philosophical background of the origins of the negative attitude to the Bible see Henning Graf Reventlow, *The Authority of the Bible and the Rise of the Modern World*, trans. John Bowden (Philadelphia: Fortress, 1985).

[2]Cited from the *Journal of the Evangelical Theological Society* 21 (1978): 289.

[3]Article 3, *Journal of the Evangelical Theological Society* 21 (1978): 290.

[4]For an account of general revelation see Bruce A. Demarest, *General Revelation: Historical Views and Contemporary Issues* (Grand Rapids: Zondervan, 1982).

[5]Recent discussions of revelation and the Bible include Stephen T. Davis, *The Debate about the Bible: Inerrancy Versus Infallibility* (Philadelphia: Westminster, 1977); Jack B. Rogers and Donald K. McKim, *The Authority and Interpretation of the Bible: An Historical Approach* (San Francisco: Harper & Row, 1979); John D. Woodbridge, *Biblical Authority: A Critique of the Rogers/McKim Proposal* (Grand Rapids: Zondervan, 1982); Norman L. Geisler, ed., *Inerrancy* (Grand Rapids: Zondervan, 1979); William J. Abraham, *Divine Revelation and the Limits of Historical Criticism* (New York: Oxford University Press, 1982); Ronald Youngblood, ed., *Evangelicals and Inerrancy* (Nashville: Nelson, 1984); Donald K. McKim, *What Christians Believe about the Bible* (Nashville: Nelson, 1985); D. A. Carson and John D. Woodbridge, eds., *Scripture and Truth* (Grand Rapids: Zondervan, 1983).

[6]*God Who Acts: Biblical Theology as Recital*, Studies in Biblical Theology, no. 8 (London: SCM, 1952), p. 55.

[7]Ibid., p. 55.

[8]Ibid.

[9]*Nature, Man and God*, Gifford Lectures 1932–1934 (London: Macmillan, 1934), p. 322.

[10]Ibid., p. 317.

[11]*Existence and Faith*, trans. Schubert M. Ogden, reprint (London: Fontana, 1964), pp. 100, 102.

[12] Ibid., p. 106; cf. Bultmann, *Jesus Christ and Mythology*, trans. Paul Schubert et al. (New York: Scribner; London: SCM, 1958), pp. 62, 64.

[13] *Existence and Faith*, p. 163; cf. Bultmann's strictures on his colleagues and scholars who have embarked on the new quest of the historical Jesus by trying to show how the kerygma of the early church is grounded in the history of Jesus: "The Primitive Christian Kerygma and the Historical Jesus" (1962), in C. E. Braaten and R. A. Harrisville, eds., *The Historical Jesus and the Kerygmatic Christ: Essays on the New Quest of the Historical Jesus* (New York: Abingdon, 1964), pp. 15–42.

[14] *Kerygma and Myth*, 1:34–44. "It is often said, most of the time in criticism, that according to my interpretation of the kerygma Jesus has risen in the kerygma. I accept this proposition. It is entirely correct, assuming that it is properly understood" (in *The Historical Jesus and the Kerygmatic Christ*, p. 42). Cf. O. Cullmann's comments in *Salvation in History* (London: SCM; Philadelphia: Westminster, 1967), pp. 50ff.

[15] *Existence and Faith*, p. 64.

[16] *Has Christianity a Revelation?* (London: SCM, 1964), p. 238.

[17] *Salvation in History*, p. 321.

[18] *Church Dogmatics*, vol. 1, pt. 1, *The Doctrine of the Word of God*, 2d ed., trans. G. W. Bromiley (Edinburgh: T. & T. Clark, 1975), p. 137.

[19] Cf. James Barr, *Old and New in Interpretation: A Study of the Two Testaments* (London: SCM, 1966), pp. 77–78.

[20] *Church Dogmatics*, vol. 1, pt. 1, pp. 137–38.

[21] Here Barth is adopting the language of John 1:1; Revelation 19:13; cf. Hebrews 1:2. He sees Jesus Christ as the Mediator of revelation (cf. Matt. 11:27–30; Luke 19:9; John 14:6–10; 1 Cor. 1:30). For a brief account of Barth's view of the threefold form of the Word of God see Colin Brown, *Karl Barth and the Christian Message* (London: Tyndale [Inter-Varsity], 1967), pp. 30–35.

[22] *Church Dogmatics*, vol. 1, pt. 1, p. 121.

[23] Ibid., p. 132.

[24] For further discussion of Barth's view of revelation see Colin Brown, *Karl Barth and the Christian Message*, pp. 30–76.

[25] Quoted from Pannenberg's "Dogmatic Theses on the Concept of Revelation" in Wolfhart Pannenberg, ed., *Revelation as History*, trans. David Granskou and Edward Quinn (London: Sheed and Ward, 1969), p. 126.

[26] *Revelation as History*, p. 127; cf. Ulrich Wilcken's essay "The Understanding of Revelation within Primitive Christianity" (ibid., pp. 55–121).

[27] See the discussion of *Heilsgeschichte* in Richard N. Soulen's excellent *Handbook of Biblical Criticism*, 2d ed., rev. (Atlanta: John Knox, 1981), p. 82.

[28] *Revelation as History*, p. 131. Cf. also Pannenberg's understanding of the significance of Jesus' resurrection as confirming and illuminating Jesus' pre-Easter activity and as inaugurating the beginning of the end of the world (*Jesus—God and Man*, pp. 66–73).

[29] In support of this point Pannenberg cites A. Alt, "Die Deutung der Weltgeschichte im Alten Testament" (*Zeitschrift für Theologie und Kirche* 56 [1959]: pp. 129–37).

[30] *Revelation as History*, pp. 132–33. Pannenberg further develops his views in relation to Hegel in "The Significance of Christianity in the Philosophy of Hegel" (*Basic Questions*, 3:144–77).

[31] *Revelation as History*, p. 135. Pannenberg argues that this holds good even though eyes may be blinded to see what is there (cf. 2 Cor. 4:4).

[32] *Revelation as History*, p. 137.

[33] Cf. Bultmann's position noted above (n. 13) with that of D. M. Baillie (*God Was in Christ: An Essay on Incarnation and Atonement* [London: Faber & Faber, 1956], pp. 30–58) and Leander E. Keck (*A Future for the Historical Jesus: The Place*

of Jesus in Preaching and Theology [Nashville: Abingdon, 1971; London: SCM], 1972).

[34] *Revelation as History*, p. 138; cf. Pannenberg's strictures on the existential position:

"Whether the decision to believe has first to guarantee the truth of the facts on which trust in Jesus Christ and the God revealed in him depends, or whether faith is rendered independent of those facts, both come ultimately to the same thing: in both cases faith depends on the believer and his decision to believe, instead of on the factual substance in whose reliability he can trust. Where faith is understood and required in this sense—as a leap of blind "decision" without further justification—it is degraded to a work of self-redemption. A faith which does not find its justification outside itself—i.e., from the thing on which it relies—remains imprisoned in its own ego and cannot be sustained" (*The Apostles' Creed in the Light of Today's Questions*, trans. Margaret Kohl [Philadelphia: Westminster; London: SCM, 1972], p. 10).

[35] *Revelation as History*, p. 139.

[36] See above, pp. 46, 98n.25.

[37] *Revelation as History*, p. 142; cf. *The Apostles' Creed in the Light*, pp. 96–115.

[38] *Revelation as History*, p. 152.

[39] Ibid., p. 153. In discussing the idea of fulfillment, Pannenberg subsequently clarified his position in a way that avoids giving the impression that the fulfillment is like finding the missing pieces of a jigsaw puzzle that fit exactly into the place formed by the existing pieces. "Rather, history has 'overtaken' promises understood in this sense" (in J. M. Robinson and J. B. Cobb, eds., *Theology as History* [New York: Harper and Row, 1967], p. 259; cf. p. 120; Pannenberg, *Basic Questions*, 1:17, 19). See also on this A. D. Galloway, *Wolfhart Pannenberg* (London: Allen & Unwin, 1973), pp. 53ff.; Jürgen Moltmann, *Theology of Hope: On the Ground and Implications of a Christian Eschatology*, trans. James W. Leitch (London: SCM; New York: Harper & Row, 1967), pp. 110ff.; J. Goldingay, "That You May Know that Yahweh is God: A Study of the Relationship between Theology and Historical Truth in the Old Testament," in *Tyndale Bulletin* 23 (1972): 58–93, see esp. p. 70; E. Schweizer, *Jesus*, trans. David E. Green (London: SCM; Richmond: John Knox, 1971), pp. 13–51; and the discussion of fulfillment above, pp. 49, 98n.34.

[40] *Revelation as History*, pp. 153–54.

[41] Ibid., p. 154.

[42] Ibid., p. 158; cf. "Kerygma and History," in *Basic Questions*, 1:81–95.

[43] H. Conzelmann, *An Outline Theology of the New Testament*, trans. John Bowden (London: SCM; New York: Harper & Row, 1969), p. 236.

[44] *Revelation as History*, pp. 150–51. On the question of Gnosticism and its possible influence on the New Testament church see R. M. Wilson, *Gnosis and the New Testament* (Philadelphia: Fortress, 1968); Edwin M. Yamauchi, *Pre-Christian Gnosticism: A Survey of the Proposed Evidence*, 2d ed. (Grand Rapids: Baker, 1983); Kurt Rudolf, *Gnosis: The Nature and History of Gnosticism*, translation ed. R. M. Wilson (San Francisco: Harper & Row, 1983); and the literature noted at the end of the article on "Knowledge" in Colin Brown, ed., *The New International Dictionary of New Testament Theology*, 3 vols. (Grand Rapids: Zondervan; Exeter: Paternoster, 1976) 2:408–9.

[45] In a performative utterance the words themselves actually bring about the action, e.g., "I name this ship the *Queen Elizabeth*." Similarly, the statement "I promise that . . ." is not a mere description but the actual making of the promise. Statements such as "I believe in God," "I baptize you in the name of the Father, and of the Son, and of the Holy Spirit," are in themselves part of the action. It would seem that statements such as "Son, your sins are forgiven . . . take your mat and walk . . ." (Mark 2:5, 10) and "The time has come. . . . The

kingdom of God is near. Repent and believe the good news" (1:15) do not merely contain descriptions but actually bring about a new state of affairs through being uttered. On this aspect of language see J. L. Austin, *Philosophical Papers*, ed. J. O. Urmson and G. J. Warnock (London: Oxford University Press, 1961), pp. 222–39; Donald D. Evans, *The Logic of Self-Involvement: A Philosophical Study of Everyday Language with Special Reference to the Christian Use of Language about God as Creator* (London: SCM, 1963).

46 *New Testament Theology*, vol. 1, *The Proclamation of Jesus*, trans. John Bowden (New York: Scribner; London: SCM, 1971), p. 96.

47 The phrase is that of E. Haenchen, endorsed by C. H. Dodd and Joachim Jeremias (Joachim Jeremias, *The Parables of Jesus*, trans. S. H. Hooke, 2d ed. [New York: Scribner; London: SCM, 1963], p. 230). See also A. C. Thieselton, "The Parables as Language-Event: Some Comments of Fuch's Hermeneutics in the Light of Linguistic Philosophy," *Scottish Journal of Theology* 23 (1970): 437–68; K. Kantzer, "The Christ-Revelation as Act and Interpretation," in Carl F. H. Henry, ed., *Jesus of Nazareth: Saviour and Lord* (Grand Rapids: Eerdmans, 1966; London: Inter-Varsity, 1967), pp. 243–64.

48 Cf. Ian T. Ramsey, *Religious Language*, pp. 11–48; Ramsey, ed., *Words about God* (London: SCM, 1971), pp. 202–23.

49 Emil Brunner, drawing on the work of F. Ebner and Martin Buber, saw Revelation as an I-Thou encounter, as opposed to an I-It relationship (Emil Brunner, *Truth as Encounter*, trans. A. M. Loos and D. Cairns [Philadelphia: Westminster; London: SCM, 1964]). The application of this concept to revelation has been criticized, but not in my opinion convincingly, by J. Macquarrie, in *Principles of Christian Theology*, rev. ed. (New York: Scribner; London: SCM, 1977), pp. 92ff.

50 See Karl Barth and Emil Brunner, *Natural Theology: Comprising "Nature and Grace" by Professor Dr. Emil Brunner and the reply "No!" by Dr. Karl Barth*, trans. Peter Fraenkel (London: Geoffrey Bles, 1946). For discussion of Barth's view see Colin Brown, *Karl Barth and the Christian Message* (London: Tyndale, 1965), pp. 77–98.

51 See, e.g., the discussion of John Wenham ("Christ's View of Scripture," in Geisler, *Inerrancy*, pp. 3–39) and B. B. Warfield (*The Inspiration and Authority of the Bible* [Philadelphia: Presbyterian and Reformed, 1948; London: Marshall, Morgan and Scott, 1951]). For responses to Warfield see David H. Kelsey, *The Uses of Scripture in Recent Theology* (Philadelphia: Fortress, 1975), esp. pp. 17–24, 28–30, 172–73; and Rogers and McKim, *Authority and Interpretation of the Bible*, pp. 323–80, who give details of further literature.

52 Brown, *Karl Barth*, pp. 34, 111–12; D. M. Baillie, *The Theology of the Sacraments and Other Papers* (London: Faber and Faber; New York: Scribner, 1957), pp. 42–47.

53 See above, pp. 48ff.

54 *Faith and Knowledge* (Ithaca, N.Y.: Cornell University Press; 2d ed., London: Macmillan, 1967), pp. 141–42; cf. Ludwig Wittgenstein, *Philosophical Investigations*, trans. G. E. M. Anscombe, 3d ed. (Oxford: Basil Blackwell, 1967), pt. 2, sec. 11, pp. 193–229e.

55 *Faith and Knowledge*, p. 103.

56 Quoted from the reprint in Ian T. Ramsey, ed., *Christian Ethics and Contemporary Philosophy* (London: SCM, 1966, pp. 53–73), p. 68.

57 *Christian Ethics*, p. 63.

58 See, e.g., the arguments of Joachim Jeremias, *The Parables of Jesus* (London: SCM; rev. ed., New York: Scribner, 1963); and Ernst Fuchs, "Bemerkungen zur Gleichnisauslegung" in *Zur Frage nach dem historischen Jesus* (Tübingen: Mohr [Siebeck], 1960), pp. 136–42.

⁵⁹Exodus 12–15; 20:2. Note the allusions to the Exodus theme in both the Old and New Testaments (Judg. 6:8–9, 13; 1 Sam. 12:6ff.; 1 Kings 8:51; 2 Chron. 7:22; Neh. 9:9ff; Pss. 77:14–20; 78:12–55; 80:8; 106:7–12; 114; Jer. 7:21–24; 11:1–8; 34:13; Dan. 9:15; Hos. 11:1; 1 Cor. 10:1ff.; Heb. 3:16ff.; 13:13).

⁶⁰*Criticism and Faith* (Nashville: Abingdon-Cokesbury, 1952; London: Hodder & Stoughton, 1953), p. 9; cf. Knox, *The Church and the Reality of Christ* (New York: Harper & Row, 1962; London: Collins, 1963), p. 16. For a contrary view see J. A. T. Robinson, *The Priority of John*, ed. J. F. Coakley (London: SCM, 1985), p. 354.

⁶¹See A. R. C. Leaney's account of the quest of the historical Jesus in recent discussion in Anthony Hanson, ed., *Vindications: Essays on the Historical Basis of Christianity* (London: SCM, 1966), pp. 103–14.

⁶²In C. Braaten and R. A. Harrisville, eds., *Kerygma and History: A Symposium on the Theology of Rudolf Bultmann* (Nashville: Abingdon, 1962), p. 107.

⁶³See, e.g., the views of G. A. Wells in his books *The Jesus of the Early Christians: A Study in Christian Origins* (London: Pemberton, 1961); *Did Jesus Exist?* (London: Elek-Pemberton, 1975); and *The Historical Evidence for Jesus* (Buffalo, N.Y.: Prometheus Books, 1982); and the somewhat less extreme position of Ian Wilson, *Jesus: The Evidence* (San Francisco: Harper & Row, 1984), which was published as a companion to a British television documentary series. Such works call in question the historical basis of Christian faith in the person of Jesus.

⁶⁴In Anthony Hanson, ed., *Vindications*, p. 72. R. P. C. Hanson has subjected to close scrutiny the undue pessimism of some modern scholars in his essay "Are We Cut Off from the Past?" (*Studies in Christian Antiquity* [Edinburgh: T. & T. Clark, 1985], pp. 3–21).

5. A Note on the Gospel Miracles

¹Reinhold Seeberg, "Wunder," *Realenzyklopädie für Protestantische Theologie und Kirche*, ed. A. Hauck (Leipzig: J. C. Hinrich'sche Buchhandlung, 1908), 21:562.

²Wilhelm Bousset, *Kyrios Christos: A History of the Belief in Christ from the Beginnings of Christianity to Irenaeus*, trans. John E. Steely (Nashville and New York: Abingdon, 1970), p. 98.

³*Kyrios Christos*, p. 100.

⁴The "divine man" idea figures in, e.g., Ludwig Bieler, *Theios Aner. Das Bild des "göttlichen Menschen" in Spätantike and Frühchristentum* (1935–36; reprint in 1 vol., Darmstadt: Wissenschaftliche Buchgesellschaft, 1976); Hans-Dieter Betz, "Jesus as Divine Man" in F. Thomas Trotter, ed., *Jesus and the Historian: Written in Honor of Ernest Cadman Colwell* (Philadelphia: Westminster, 1978), pp. 114–33; Rudolf Bultmann, *Theology of the New Testament*, 1:130–31; 2:42ff.; Theodore J. Weeden, Sr., *Mark: Traditions in Conflict* (Philadelphia: Fortress, 1971; reprint with new preface, 1979); Dieter Georgi, "Socioeconomic Reasons for the 'Divine Man' as a Propagandistic Pattern," in Elisabeth Schüssler Fiorenza, ed., *Aspects of Religious Propaganda in Judaism and Early Christianity* (Notre Dame: University of Notre Dame Press, 1976), pp. 27–42.

In recent years the concept of the "divine man" has been subjected to close scrutiny. Many scholars would now say that the notion of the "divine man" is a hypothetical composite picture and that there was no single type of "divine man" in antiquity. The term might simply denote a wise, virtuous man. Moses qualified for the designation in view of his being an agent of God's power and purpose. Miracle working, however, was not generally linked with the idea of the "divine man." For critical discussions see David Lenz Tiede, *The Charismatic*

Figure as Miracle Worker, Society of Biblical Literature Dissertation Series 1 (Missoula: Society of Biblical Literature, 1972); Carl H. Holladay, *Theios Aner in Hellenistic Judaism: A Critique of the Use of this Category in New Testament Christology*, Society of Biblical Literature Dissertation Series 40 (Missoula: Scholars, 1977); W. L. Lane, "Theios Aner Christology and the Gospel of Mark," in Richard N. Longenecker and Merrill C. Tenney, eds., *New Dimensions in New Testament Study* (Grand Rapids: Zondervan, 1974), pp. 144–61; Howard Clark Kee, *Miracles in the Early Christian World: A Study in Sociohistorical Method* (New Haven: Yale University Press, 1983), pp. 297–99; Barry L. Blackburn, " 'Miracle Working *Theioi Andres*' in Hellenism, (and Hellenistic Judaism)," in David Wenham and Craig Blomberg, *Gospel Perspectives*, vol. 6, *The Miracles of Jesus* (Sheffield: JSOT, 1986), pp. 185–218; Eugene V. Gallagher, *Divine Man or Magician? Celsus and Origen on Jesus*, Society of Biblical Literature Dissertation Series 64 (Chico, Calif.: Scholars, 1982). In the reissue of his book that saw the "divine man" idea at the root of conflict over Jesus, Weeden conceded that the category may prove unsatisfactory for describing the christology and discipleship of Mark's opponents (T. J. Weeden, Sr., *Mark*, p. vii).

[5]Morton Smith, *Jesus the Magician* (San Francisco: Harper & Row, 1978). Others who have examined the question of magic and the Gospels include John M. Hull, *Hellenistic Magic and the Synoptic Tradition*, Studies in Biblical Theology, 2d. ser., no. 28 (London: SCM, 1974); and David E. Aune, "Magic in Early Christianity," in H. Temporini and W. Haase, eds., *Aufstieg und Niedergang der römischen Welt* (Berlin: Walter de Gruyter, 1980), pt. 2, vol. 23, pt. 2, pp. 1507–57. For a judicious review of the views of these and other scholars see Edwin Yamauchi, "Magic or Miracle? Diseases, Demons and Exorcisms," in David Wenham and Craig Blomberg, eds., *The Miracles of Jesus*, pp. 89–183.

[6]Colin Brown, "Synoptic Miracle Stories: A Jewish Religious and Social Setting," *Foundations & Facets Forum* 2 (1986): 1–21.

[7]*Institutes of the Christian Religion*, Prefatory Address to King Francis I of France (1536), The Library of Christian Classics, ed. J. T. McNeill, trans. F. L. Battles (Philadelphia: Westminster; London: SCM, 1960), pp. 17–18. See further my discussion of Calvin in *Miracles and the Critical Mind* (Grand Rapids: Eerdmans; Exeter: Paternoster, 1984), pp. 15–18.

[8]Benjamin B. Warfield, *Miracles: Yesterday and Today, True and False* (originally published under the title *Counterfeit Miracles* [New York: Scribner, 1918]; Grand Rapids: Eerdmans, 1954), p. 122. For discussion of Warfield see Brown, *Miracles*, pp. 64–68, 198–204, and passim.

[9]Diviners, wizards, sorcerers, and sundry other practitioners of abominations shall not be found in the land, for the people are to be blameless before the Lord (Deut. 18:10–14). The presumptuous prophet who speaks falsely in God's name will die (Deut. 18:20–22), as will the "rebellious son" who refuses to hear the voice of his father or mother (Deut. 21:18–21; cf. Exod. 20:12; Deut. 5:16; 27:16). The rebellious son is to be purged from the midst of the people. The convicted person who is put to death by being hanged on a tree is under the curse of God (Deut. 21:22–23; cf. Gal. 3:13). He is to be buried the same day to avoid defiling the land. The practitioners of magic in any form are to be put to death (Exod. 22:18; Lev. 19:26, 31; 20:6, 27).

For a brief account and literature on the subject see Colin Brown and J. Stafford Wright, "Magic, Sorcery, Magi," in Colin Brown, ed., *The New International Dictionary of New Testament Theology*, 3 vols. with index (Grand Rapids: Zondervan; Exeter: Paternoster, 1975–85), 2:552–62. On the accusations against Jesus both before and at his trial see Ethelbert Stauffer, *Jerusalem und Rom im Zeitalter Jesu* (Bern: Francke Verlag, 1957); Stauffer, *Jesus and His Story*, English trans. by Dorothea M. Barton (London: SCM, 1960); American trans. by Richard and Clara Winston (New York: Knopf, 1960); August Strobel,

Die Stunde der Wahrheit. Untersuchungen zum Strafverfahren gegen Jesu, Wissenschaftliche Untersuchungen zum Neuen Testament, vol. 21 (Tübingen: Mohr [Siebeck], 1980).

[10] *Jesus and His Story*, p. 74.

[11] *Dialogue with Trypho*, 108.

[12] See Geza Vermes, *Jesus the Jew: A Historian's Reading of the Gospels* (London: Collins, 1969), pp. 58–82, where Vermes seeks to show that Jesus was really a Galilean charismatic figure in the same tradition as Honi and Hanina ben Dosa. See further Geza Vermes, *Jesus and the World of Judaism* (Philadelphia: Fortress, 1984), pp. 5–11; and his more detailed study of "Hanina ben Dosa" in G. Vermes, *Post-Biblical Jewish Studies, Studies in Judaism in Late Antiquity*, no. 8 (Leiden: E. J. Brill, 1975), pp. 178–214.

[13] On this question see Yamauchi, "Magic or Miracle?"

[14] In general the New Testament speaks in the passive about Jesus' resurrection. It is not some action he did or initiated; it is something that was done to him. The writers use language like that of God raising him (Acts 10:40), raising him up (Acts 2:24), raising him from the dead (Acts 4:10; cf. Gal. 1:1; Heb. 13:20). Paul could use the simple passive "he was raised" (1 Cor. 15:4; cf. 15:12–14) and "raised from the dead" (1 Cor. 15:20). In Romans 1:4 Paul says that Jesus "through the Spirit of holiness was declared with power to be the Son of God by his resurrection from the dead." In the light of the condemnation of Jesus by the Sanhedrin, the Resurrection is thus the vindication of Jesus.

The same may be said of John 2:19: "Destroy this temple, and I will raise it again in three days" (cf. also v. 22). Even in this passage it is not a case of Jesus' personal divinity being the ground of his resurrection. The pronouncement signifies God's reversal of man's verdict. Moreover, Jesus' words and actions are presented in John as the words and actions of the Father (John 8:28, 38; 10:18; 12:49–50; 14:10; 17:8). Nothing, according to John's portrayal of Jesus, is the word or action of Jesus alone; rather, all things are the word or action of the Father spoken or performed by him.

Select Bibliography

1. The Philosophy of History and General Works

Atkinson, R. F. *Knowledge and Explanation in History: An Introduction to the Philosophy of History.* Ithaca, N.Y.: Cornell University Press, 1978.

Austin, J. L. *Philosophical Papers.* Ed. J. O. Urmson and G. J. Warnock. London: Oxford University Press, 1961.

Ausubel, Herman. *Historians and Their Craft: A Study of the Presidential Addresses of the American Historical Association.* New York: Oxford University Press, 1950.

Barbour, Ian G. *Issues in Science and Religion.* Englewood Cliffs, N.J.: Prentice-Hall, 1966; London: SCM, 1968.

_____. *Myths, Models and Paradigms: The Nature of Scientific and Religious Language.* New York: Harper & Row; London: SCM, 1974.

Barnes, Harry Elmer. *A History of Historical Writing.* Norman, Okla.: University of Oklahoma Press, 1937.

Barraclough, Geoffrey. *History in a Changing World.* London: Oxford University Press, 1955. Reprint. Norman, Okla.: University of Oklahoma, n.d.

Barzun, Jacques, and Graff, Henry F. *The Modern Researcher.* Rev. ed. New York: Harcourt, Brace and World, 1970.

Bauer, Gerhard. *"Geschichtlichkeit": Wege und Irrwege eines Begriffs.* Berlin: Walter de Gruyter, 1963.

Becker, Carl L. *Detachment and the Writing of History: Essays and Letters of Carl L. Becker.* Ed. P. Snyder. Ithaca, N.Y.: Cornell University Press, 1958.

_____. *The Heavenly City of the Eighteenth-Century Philosophers.* New Haven: Yale University Press, 1932.

Berlin, Sir Isaiah. *Historical Inevitability.* London: Oxford University Press, 1954.

Black, J. B. *The Art of History: A Study of Four Great Historians of the Eighteenth Century.* New York: Russell and Russell, 1965.

Black, Max. *Models and Metaphors: Studies in Language and Philosophy.* Ithaca, N.Y.: Cornell University Press, 1962.

Bloch, M. *The Historian's Craft.* Trans. Peter Putnam. Manchester: Manchester University Press, 1954.

Braithwaite, R. B. *Scientific Explanation.* Cambridge: Cambridge University Press, 1953.

Breisach, Ernst. *Historiography, Ancient, Medieval and Modern.* Chicago: University of Chicago Press, 1983.

Butterfield, Sir Herbert. *History and Human Relations.* London: Collins, 1951.

_____. *Man on His Past: The Study of the History of Historical Scholarship.* Cambridge: Cambridge University Press, 1955.

Cancik, Hubert. *Mythische und historische Wahrheit.* Stuttgarter Bibelstudien, no. 48. Stuttgart: Katholisches Bibelwerk, 1970.

Carr, E. H. *What is History?* Trevelyan Lectures 1961. London: Macmillan, 1961. Paperback. Harmondsworth: Pelican, 1964.

Clark, Gordon H. *Historiography: Secular and Religious.* Nutley, N.J.: Craig, 1971.

Cohen, Gerard A. *Karl Marx's Theory of History: A Defence.* Princeton: Princeton University Press, 1978.

Collingwood, R. G. *Human Nature and Human History.* London: Oxford University Press, for the British Academy, 1936.

————. *The Idea of History.* London: Oxford University Press, 1946. Reprinted with alterations, 1961.

Commager, Henry Steele. *The Nature and Study of History.* Columbus, Ohio: Charles E. Merrill Publishing Co., 1965.

Croce, Bendetto. *Theory and History of Historiography.* Trans. D. Ainslie. London: Harrap, 1921.

Dance, E. H. *History the Betrayer.* 2d ed. London: Hutchinson, 1964.

Danto, Arthur C. *Analytical Philosophy and History.* Cambridge: Cambridge University Press, 1965.

D'Arcy, M. C. *The Sense of History, Secular and Sacred.* London: Faber and Faber, 1959.

Davis, R. H. C., and Wallace-Hadrill, J. M., with the assistance of R. J. A. I. Catto and M. H. Keen. *The Writing of History in the Middle Ages: Essays Presented to Richard William Southern.* Oxford: Clarendon, 1981.

Dilthey, W. *Gesammelte Schriften,* 19 vols. Reprint. Stuttgart: B. G. Teubner; Göttingen: Vandenhoeck & Ruprecht, 1959–82. 7. *Der Aufbau der geschictlichen Welt in den Geisteswissenschaften;* 8. *Weltanschauungslehre: Abhandlungen zur Philosophie der Philosophie.* Leipzig: Teubner, 1931.

————. *Pattern and Meaning in History: Thoughts on History and Society.* New York: Harper & Row, 1961.

————. *Selected Works.* Ed. Rudolf A. Makkreel and Frithjot Rodi. 6 vols. Princeton: Princeton University Press, 1985–.

Donagan, Alan. *The Later Philosophy of R. G. Collingwood.* London: Oxford University Press, 1962.

Donagan, Alan, and Donagan, Barbara. *Philosophy of History.* New York: Macmillan, 1965.

Dray, William. *Philosophy of History.* Englewood Cliffs, N.J.: Prentice-Hall, 1964.

————. "History and Value Judgments." *Encyclopedia of Philosophy.* 6:247–54.

Dray, William, ed. *Philosophical Analysis and History.* New York: Harper & Row, 1966.

Edwards, Paul, editor-in-chief. *The Encyclopedia of Philosophy.* 8 vols. New York: Macmillan; London: Collier Macmillan, 1967.

Elton, G. R. *The Practice of History.* Paperback. London: Fontana Books, 1969.

Ermath, Michael. *Wilhelm Dilthey: The Critique of Historical Reason.* Chicago: University of Chicago Press, 1978.

Finberg, H. P. R., ed. *Approaches to History: A Symposium.* Toronto: University of Toronto Press, 1962.

Flew, Antony, editorial consultant. *A Dictionary of Philosophy.* Rev. 2d ed. New York: St. Martin's, 1984.

Gadamer, Hans-Georg. *Truth and Method*. Translation ed. Garrett Barden and John Cumming. New York: Seabury; London: Sheed and Ward, 1975.

Gallie, W. B. *Philosophy and the Historical Understanding*. London: Chatto & Windus, 1964.

Galston, William A. *Kant and the Problem of History*. Chicago: University of Chicago Press, 1975.

Gardiner, Patrick. *The Nature of Historical Explanation*. Paperback. London: Oxford University Press, 1968.

Gardiner, Patrick, ed. *Theories of History*. Glencoe, Ill.: Free, 1959.

Geyl, Pieter, *Debates with Historians*. Paperback. London: Fontana, 1970.

―――. *Use and Abuse of History*. Reprint. Hamden, Conn.: Archon, 1970.

Gillespie, Michael Allen. *Hegel, Heidegger and the Ground of History*. Chicago: University of Chicago Press, 1984.

Gooch, G. P. *History and Historians in the Nineteenth Century*. 2d ed. London: Longmans, 1952.

Halperin, S. W., ed. *Some 20th-Century Historians*. Chicago: University of Chicago Press, 1961.

Heussi, Karl. *Die Krisis des Historismus*. Tübingen: J. C. B. Mohr (Paul Siebeck), 1932.

Hexter, Jack H. *Doing History*. Bloomington, Ind.: Indiana University Press; London: Allen & Unwin, 1971.

―――. *The History Primer*. Harmondsworth: Allen Lane, Penguin, 1972.

―――. *Reappraisals in History*. Evanston: Northwestern University Press; London: Longmans, 1961.

Hook, Sidney, ed. *Philosophy and History: A Symposium*. New York: New York University Press, 1963.

Hughes, H. Stuart. *History as Art and as Science*. New York: Harper & Row, 1964.

Huizinga, Johan. *Men and Ideas: History, the Middle Ages, the Renaissance*. Princeton: Princeton University Press, 1984.

Hume, David. *Enquiries Concerning the Human Understanding and Concerning Principles of Morals*. Ed. L. A. Selby-Bigge. 3d ed. Rev. P. H. Nidditch. Oxford: Clarendon, 1975.

Johnson, Allen. *The Historian and Historical Existence*. New York: Scribner, 1934.

Kant, Immanuel. *Critique of Pure Reason*. Trans. Norman Kemp Smith. Paperback. London: Macmillan, 1973.

―――. *Foundations of the Metaphysics of Morals and What is Enlightenment?* Trans. Lewis White Beck. Paperback. Indianapolis and New York: Bobbs-Merrill, 1959.

―――. *Religion within the Limits of Reason Alone*. Trans. with an introduction and notes by Theodore M. Greene and Hoyt H. Hudson. Includes a new essay entitled "The Ethical Significance of Kant's *Religion*" by John R. Silber. Paperback. New York: Harper & Row, 1960.

Kellner, Hans, et al. *Metahistory: Six Critiques*. History and Theory: Studies in the Philosophy of History. Beiheft 19. Middletown, Conn.: Wesleyan University Press, 1980.

Klibansky, R., and Paton, H. J., eds. *Philosophy and History: Essays Presented to Ernst Cassirer*. Oxford: Oxford University Press, 1936.

Knowles, Dom David. *The Historian and Character, and Other Essays*. Cambridge: Cambridge University Press, 1963.

Kracauer, Siegfried. *History: The Last Things before the Last*. New York: Oxford University Press, 1969.

Krausz, Michael, ed. *Critical Essays on the Philosophy of R. G. Collingwood*. Oxford: Clarendon, 1972.

Kren, George M., and Rappoport, Leon H., eds. *Varieties of Psychohistory*. New York: Springer, 1976.

Krieger, William A., et al. *Essays on Historians*. History and Theory: Studies in the Philosophy of History. Beiheft 14. Middletown, Conn.: Wesleyan University Press, 1975.

LaCapra, Dominick. *History and Criticism*. Ithaca, N.Y.: Cornell University Press, 1985.

Lewis, Bernard. *History: Remembered, Recorded, Invented*. Princeton: Princeton University Press, 1976.

Löwith, Karl. *Meaning in History: The Theological Implications of the Philosophy of History*. Chicago: University of Chicago Press, 1949.

Lukacs, John. *Historical Consciousness or the Remembered Past*. New York: Schocken Books, 1985.

MacCormac, Earl R. *Metaphor and Myth in Science and Religion*. Durham, N.C.: Duke University Press, 1976.

Mandelbaum, Maurice. *The Anatomy of Historical Knowledge*. Baltimore: Johns Hopkins University Press, 1977.

———. "Historicism." *Encyclopedia of Philosophy*. 4:22–25.

———. *The Problem of Historical Knowledge: An Answer to Relativism*. New York: Harper & Row, 1938.

Maritain, Jacques. *On the Philosophy of History*. Ed. Joseph W. Evans. New York: Scribner, 1957.

Marwick, Arthur. *The Nature of History*. London: Macmillan, for the Open University, 1970.

Mazlish, Bruce. *The Riddle of History: The Great Speculators from Vico to Freud*. New York: Harper & Row, 1966.

Mehta, Ved. *Fly and the Fly-Bottle: Encounters with British Intellectuals*. Harmondsworth: Pelican Books, 1965.

Meiland, Jack W. *Scepticism and Historical Knowledge*. New York: Random House, 1965.

Meinecke, Friedrich. *Historicism: The Rise of a New Outlook*. Trans. J. E. Anderson and M. D. Schmidt. London: Routledge & Kegan Paul, 1972.

———. *Zur Geschichte der Geschichtsschreibung*. Munich: Koehler, 1968.

———. *Zur Theorie und Philosophie der Geschichte*. 2d ed. Munich: Koehler, 1965.

Meyerhoff, H., ed. *The Philosophy of History in our Time: An Anthology*. Garden City: Doubleday, 1959.

Mohan, R. P. *Philosophy of History: An Introduction*. New York: Bruce Publishing Company, 1970.

Momigliano, Arnaldo, et al. *History and the Concept of Time*. History and Theory. Studies in the Philosophy of History. Beiheft 6. Middletown, Conn.: Wesleyan University Press, 1966.

Murphey, Murray G. *Our Knowledge of the Historical Past.* Indianapolis and New York: Bobbs-Merrill, 1973.

Nadel, George H. *Studies in the Philosophy of History: Selected Essays from History and Theory.* New York: Harper & Row, 1965.

Namier, Sir Lewis. *Avenues of History.* London: Hamish Hamilton, 1952.

———. *Personalities and Powers.* London: Hamish Hamilton, 1955.

Nash, Ronald H. *Ideas of History.* 2 vols. New York: E. P. Dutton, 1969.

Oakeshott, Maurice. *Experience and its Modes.* Cambridge: Cambridge University Press, 1933.

Olafson, Fredrick A. *The Dialetic of Action: A Philosophical Interpretation of History and the Humanities.* Chicago: University of Chicago Press, 1979.

Oman, Sir Charles. *On the Writing of History.* London: Methuen, 1939.

Peacocke, A. R. *Science and the Christian Experiment.* London: Oxford University Press, 1971.

Pflug, G., et al. *Enlightenment Historiography: Three German Studies.* History and Theory. Studies in the Philosophy of History. Beiheft 11. Middletown, Conn.: Wesleyan University Press, 1971.

Plantinga, Theodore. *Historical Understanding in the Thought of Wilhelm Dilthey.* Toronto: University of Toronto Press, 1980.

Plumb, J. H. *The Death of the Past.* London: Macmillan, 1969. Paperback. Harmondsworth: Pelican Books, 1973.

Polanyi, Michael. *Personal Knowledge: Towards a Post-critical Philosophy.* London: Routledge & Kegan Paul; Chicago: University of Chicago Press, 1958.

———. *The Tacit Dimension.* Garden City, N.Y.: Doubleday, 1966; London: Routledge & Kegan Paul, 1967.

Pomper, Philip. *The Structure of the Mind in History: Five Major Figures in Psychohistory.* New York: Columbia University Press, 1985.

Popkin, Richard H. *The History of Skepticism from Erasmus to Spinoza.* Berkeley, Los Angeles, London: University of California Press, 1979.

Popper, Sir Karl. *The Poverty of Historicism.* London: Routledge & Kegan Paul; Boston: Beacon, 1957.

Press, Gerald A. *The Development of the Idea of History in Antiquity.* Kingston and Montreal: McGill-Queen's University Press, 1982.

Price, H. H. *Belief.* London: Allen & Unwin, 1969.

———. *Thinking and Experience.* London: Hutchinson, 1953.

Rickmann, Hans Peter. *Wilhelm Dilthey: Pioneer of the Human Studies.* Berkeley, Los Angeles, London: University of California Press, 1979.

Rotenstreich, Nathan. *Philosophy, History and Politics: Studies in Contemporary English Philosophy of History.* The Hague: Martinus Nijhoff, 1976.

Rowse, A. L. *The Use of History.* Paperback. Harmondsworth: Pelican Books, 1963.

Schilpp, P. A., ed. *The Philosophy of Ernst Cassirer.* La Salle, Ill.: Open Court, 1949.

Simmel, Georg. *The Problems of the Philosophy of History: An Epistemological Essay.* Trans. Guy Oates. New York: Free, 1977.

Skotheim, Robert Allen. *American Intellectual Histories and Historians*. Princeton: Princeton University Press, 1966.

Smith, Page. *The Historian and History*. Paperback. New York: Random House, Vintage Books, 1966.

Spinoza, Benedict de. *A Theologico-Political Treatise and A Political Treatise*. Trans. R. H. M. Elwes. Paperback. New York: Dover Books, 1951.

———. *On the Improvement of the Understanding; The Ethics; Correspondence*. Trans. R. H. M. Elwes. Paperback. New York: Dover Books, 1955.

Stannard, David E. *Shrinking History: On Freud and the Failure of Psycho-history*. New York: Oxford University Press, 1980.

Stern, Fritz, ed. *The Varities of History: From Voltaire to the Present*. 2d ed. New York and London: Macmillan, 1970.

Stover, Robert. *The Nature of Historical Thinking*. Chapel Hill: University of North Carolina, 1967.

Thompson, James Westfall, in collaboration with Bernard J. Hokm. *History of Historical Writing*. 2 vols. New York: Macmillan, 1942. Reprint. Gloucester, Mass.: Peter Smith, 1967.

Trompf, G. W. *The Idea of Historical Recurrence in Western Thought from Antiquity to the Reformation*. Berkeley, Los Angeles, London: University of California Press, 1979.

Voegelin, Eric. *Anamnesis*. Trans. and ed. Gerhart Niemeyer. Notre Dame: University of Notre Dame Press, 1978.

Wagner, Fritz, ed. *Geschichtswissenschaft*. Munich: Karl Alber Verlag, 1966.

Walsh, W. H. *An Introduction to the Philosophy of History*. London: Hutchinson, 1951.

White, M. *Foundations of Historical Knowledge*. New York: Harper & Row, 1956.

Widgery, A. G. *The Meanings in History*. London: Allen & Unwin, 1967.

Wilkins, Burleigh Taylor. *Has History any Meaning? A Critique of Popper's Philosophy of History*. Ithaca, N.Y.: Cornell University Press, 1978.

Wittgenstein, Ludwig. *Philosophical Investigations*. German text with English trans. by G. E. M. Anscombe. 3d ed. Oxford: Basil Blackwell, 1967.

———. *Tractatus Logico-Philosophicus*. Trans. D. F. Pears and B. F. McGuiness. New York: Humanities; London: Routledge & Kegan Paul, 1961.

Wolman, Benjamin, ed. *The Psychoanalytic Interpretation of History*. New York, London: Basic Books, 1971.

2. History and Christianity

Abrahams, William J. *Divine Revelation and the Limits of Historical Criticism*. New York: Oxford University Press, 1982.

Arbaugh, G. E., and Arbaugh, G. B. *Kierkegaard's Authorship: A Guide to the Writings of Kierkegaard*. London: Allen & Unwin, 1968.

Albright, W. F. *History, Archaeology and Christian Humanism*. New York: McGraw-Hill, 1964.

Alt, Albrecht. "Die Deutung der Weltgeschichte im Alten Testament." *Zeitschrift für Theologie und Kirche* 56 (1959) 129–37.

Anderson, Hugh. *Jesus and Christian Origins: A Commentary on Modern Viewpoints*. New York: Oxford University Press, 1964.

Anderson, J. N. D. *Christianity: The Witness of History*. London: Inter-Varsity, 1969.

Aune, David E., "Magic in Early Christianity," in H. Temporini and W. Haase, eds., *Aufstieg und Niedergang der römischen Welt*. Pt. 2, vol. 23, pt. 2. Berlin and New York: Walter de Gruyter, 1980, pp. 1507–57.

Baillie, D. M. *God Was In Christ. An Essay on Incarnation and Atonement*. London: Faber and Faber; New York: Scribner, 1948.

———. *The Theology of the Sacraments and Other Papers*. London: Faber and Faber; New York: Scribner, 1957.

Bammel, Ernst, and Moule, C. F. D., eds. *Jesus and the Politics of His Day*. Cambridge: Cambridge University Press, 1984.

Barr, James. *Old and New in Interpretation: A Study of the Two Testaments*. London: SCM, 1972.

Barth, Karl. *Church Dogmatics*. Vol. 1, pt. 1. *The Doctrine of the Word of God*. Trans. G. W. Bromiley. Edinburgh: T. & T. Clark, 1975.

———. *The Epistle to the Romans*. Trans. Sir Edwyn Hoskyns. London: Oxford University Press, 1933.

———. *Protestant Theology in the Nineteenth Century: Its Background and History*. Trans. Brian Cozens, John Bowden, et al. London: SCM, 1972.

———, and Brunner, Emil. *Natural Theology: Comprising "Nature and Grace" by Professor Dr. Emil Brunner and the Reply "No!" by Dr. Karl Barth*. Trans. Peter Fraenkel. London: Geoffrey Bles, 1946.

Bartsch, Hans-Werner, ed. *Kerygma and Myth*. Trans. Reginald H. Fuller. Vols. 1, 2. Enl. bibliography. London: SPCK, 1972.

Berkhof, Hendrikus. *Christ, the Meaning of History*. Trans. Lambertus Buurman. London: SCM, 1966.

Bieler, Ludwig. *Theios Aner. Das Bild des "göttlichen Menschen" in Spätantike und Frühchristentum*. 2 vols. 1935–36. Reprint in 1 vol. Darmstadt: Wissenschaftliche Buchgesellschaft, 1976.

Bodenstein, Walter. *Neige des Historismus: Ernst Troeltschs Entwicklungsgang*. Gütersloh: Gütersloher Verlagshaus, 1959.

Bornkamm, Günther. *Jesus of Nazareth*. Trans. Irene McLuskey and Fraser McLuskey with James M. Robinson. New York: Harper; London: Hodder & Stoughton, 1960.

Bousset, Wilhelm. *Kyrios Christos: A History of the Belief in Christ from the Beginnings to Irenaeus*. Trans. John E. Steely. Nashville and New York: Abingdon, 1970.

Braaten, Carl E. *The Historical Jesus and the Kerygmatic Christ: Essays on the New Quest of the Historical Jesus*. New York and Nashville: Abingdon, 1964.

———. *History and Hermeneutics*. Philadelphia: Westminster, 1966; London: Lutterworth, 1968.

Braaten, Carl E., and Harrisville, Roy A., eds. *Kerygma and History*. New York and Nashville: Abingdon, 1962.

Braithwaite, R. B. "An Empiricist's Approach to the Nature of Religious Belief." 1955. Reprinted in Ian T. Ramsey, ed. *Christian Ethics and Contemporary Philosophy*. London: SCM, 1966, pp. 53–73.

Brown, Colin. "Bultmann Revisited." *The Churchman* 88 (1974): 167–87.

_____. *Jesus in European Protestant Thought, 1778–1860.* Studies in Historical Theology 1. Durham, N.C.: Labyrinth, 1985.

_____. *Karl Barth and the Christian Message.* London: Tyndale, 1967.

_____. *Miracles and the Critical Mind.* Grand Rapids: Eerdmans; Exeter: Paternoster, 1984.

_____. *Philosophy and the Christian Faith: A Historical Sketch from the Middle Ages to the Present Day.* London and Downers Grove: InterVarsity, 1969.

_____. "Synoptic Miracle Stories: A Jewish Religious and Social Setting." *Foundations & Facets Forum* 2 (1986): 1–21.

_____. *That You May Believe: Miracles and Faith—Then and Now.* Grand Rapids: Eerdmans; Exeter: Paternoster, 1985.

Brown, Colin, ed. *The New International Dictionary of New Testament Theology.* 3 vols. with index vol. Grand Rapids: Zondervan; Exeter: Paternoster, 1975–85.

_____, ed. *History, Criticism and Faith: Four Explanatory Studies.* Leicester and Downers Grove: InterVarsity, 1976.

Bruce, F. F. "History and the Gospel." *Faith and Thought* 93 (1964): 121–45.

_____. *Jesus and Christian Origins Outside the New Testament.* London: Hodder & Stoughton; Grand Rapids: Eerdmans, 1974.

_____. *New Testament History.* London: Nelson; Garden City: Doubleday, 1969.

_____. *This Is That: The New Testament Development of Some Old Testament Themes.* Exeter: Paternoster; Grand Rapids: Eerdmans, 1968.

_____. *The Time is Fulfilled: Five Aspects of Fulfillment in the New Testament.* Exeter: Paternoster; Grand Rapids: Eerdmans, 1978.

_____. "When Is a Gospel Not a Gospel?" *Bulletin of the John Rylands Library* 45 (1963): 319–39.

Brunner, Emil. *Truth as Encounter.* Trans. A. M. Loos and D. Cairns. Philadelphia: Westminster; London: SCM, 1964.

Bultmann, Rudolf. *Essays Philosophical and Theological.* Trans. J. C. C. Greig. London: SCM; New York: Macmillan, 1955.

_____. *Existence and Faith: Shorter Writings.* Trans. Schubert M. Ogden. Paperback. London: Fontana, 1964.

_____. *Faith and Understanding: Collected Essays.* Ed. Robert W. Funk, trans. Louise Pettibone Smith. London: SCM, 1969.

_____. *History and Eschatology: The Presence of Eternity.* Gifford Lectures 1955. Edinburgh: Edinburgh University Press; New York: Harper & Row, 1957.

_____. *Jesus Christ and Mythology.* Trans. Paul Schubert et al. New York: Scribner; London: SCM, 1960.

_____. *New Testament and Mythology and Other Basic Writings.* Ed. and trans. Schubert M. Ogden. Philadelphia: Fortress, 1984.

_____. *Primitive Christianity in its Contemporary Setting.* Trans. R. H. Fuller. Paperback. London: Fontana Books, 1962.

Burns, R. M. *The Great Debate on Miracles: From Joseph Glanvill to David Hume.* Lewisburg: Bucknell University Press; London and Toronto: Associated University Presses, 1981.

Butterfield, Sir Herbert. *Christianity and History.* London: Bell, 1949.

———. *Writings on Christianity and History.* Ed. C. T. McIntyre. New York: Oxford University Press, 1979.

Caird, G. B. *The Language and Imagery of the Bible.* Philadelphia: Westminster, 1980.

Calvin, John. *Institutes of the Christian Religion.* Ed. J. T. McNeill, trans. Ford Lewis Battles. 2 vols. Library of Christian Classics 20–21. Philadelphia: Westminster; London: SCM, 1961.

Campbell, R. "Lessing's Problem and Kierkegaard's Answer." *SJT* 19(1966):34–54. Reprinted in J. Gill, ed., *Essays on Kierkegaard.* Minneapolis: Burgess, 1968.

———. "History and Bultmann's Structural Inconsistency." *Religious Studies* 19 (1973): 63–79.

The Cambridge History of the Bible. 3 vols. Cambridge: Cambridge University Press, 1963–70. 1. *From the Beginnings to Jerome.* Ed. P. R. Ackroyd and C. F. Evans. 1970. 2. *The West from the Fathers to the Reformation.* Ed. G. W. H. Lampe. 1969. 3. *The West from the Reformation to the Present Day.* Ed. S. L. Greenslade. 1963.

Campenhausen, Hans von. *Tradition and Life in the Church: Essays and Lectures in Church History.* Trans. A. V. Littledale. London: A. & C. Black, 1968.

Carnell, Edward John. *The Burden of Søren Kierkegaard.* Grand Rapids: Eerdmans; Exeter: Paternoster, 1965.

Carson, D. A., and Woodbridge, John D., eds., *Scripture and Truth.* Grand Rapids: Zondervan, 1983.

Casserley, J. V. L. *Toward a Theology of History.* London: Faber and Faber, 1965.

Chilton, Bruce D. *A Galilean Rabbi and His Bible: Jesus' Use of the Interpreted Scripture of His Time.* Good News Studies, no. 8. Wilmington, Del.: Michael Glazier, 1984.

Clayton, John Powell, ed. *Ernst Troeltsch and the Future of Theology.* Cambridge: Cambridge University Press, 1976.

Conzelmann, Hans. *An Outline Theology of the New Testament.* Trans. John Bowden. London: SCM; New York: Harper & Row, 1969.

Craig, William Lane. *The Historical Argument for the Resurrection of Jesus During the Deist Controversy.* Texts and Studies in Religion, no. 23. Lewiston and Queenston: Edwin Mellon, 1985.

Crites, Stephen, *In the Twilight of Christendom: Hegel vs. Kierkegaard on Faith and History.* American Academy of Religion Studies in Religion, no. 2. Chambersburg, Pa.: American Academy of Religion.

Cullmann, Oscar. *Salvation in History.* Trans. Sidney G. Sowers et al. London: SCM; New York: Harper & Row, 1967.

Davis, Stephen T. *The Debate about the Bible: Inerrancy Versus Infallibility.* Philadelphia: Westminster, 1977.

Demarest, Bruce A. *General Revelation: Historical Views and Contemporary Issues.* Grand Rapids: Zondervan, 1982.

Dodd, C. H. *The Founder of Christianity.* Paperback. London: Fontana Books, 1973.

———. *History and the Gospel.* 2d ed. London: Hodder & Stoughton, 1964.

Dupré, Louis. *Kierkegaard as Theologian.* London and New York: Sheed & Ward, 1964.

Dyson, A. O. *The Immortality of the Past*. London: SCM, 1974.

Ebeling, Gerhard. *The Nature of Faith*. Trans. Ronald Gregor Smith. Philadelphia: Muhlenberg, 1961. Paperback. London: Fontana Books, 1966.

―――. *Word and Faith*. Trans. James W. Leitch. Philadelphia: Fortress; London: SCM, 1963.

Efird, J. M., ed.. *The Use of the Old Testament in the New and Other Essays*. Durham, N.C.: Duke University Press, 1972.

Ellis, E. Earle. *Paul's Use of the Old Testament*. Edinburgh: Oliver & Boyd, 1957.

―――. *Prophecy and Hermeneutic in Early Christianity: New Testament Essays*. Wissenschaftliche Untersuchungen zum Neuen Testament. 2. Riehe 18. Tübingen: J. C. B. Mohr (Paul Siebeck), 1978.

Evans, C. F. *Resurrection and the New Testament*. Studies in Biblical Theology. 2d ser., no. 12. London: SCM, 1970.

Evans, C. Stephen. *Kierkegaard's "Fragments" and "Postscript": The Religious Philosophy of Johannes Climacus*. Atlantic Highlands, N.J.: Humanities, 1983.

Evans, D. D. *The Logic of Self-Involvement: A Philosophical Study of Everyday Language with Special Reference to the Christian Use of Language about God as Creator*. London: SCM, 1963.

Farmer, H. H. *The World and God: A Study of Prayer, Providence and Miracle in Christian Experience*. 2d ed. London: Nisbet, 1935.

Farmer, W. R., Moule, C. F. D., and Niebuhr, R. R., eds. *Christian History and Interpretation: Studies Presented to John Knox*. Cambridge: Cambridge University Press, 1967.

Flew, Antony, and MacIntyre, Alasdair, eds. *New Essays in Philosophical Theology*. London: SCM, 1955.

Flückiger, F. *Theologie der Geschichte: Die biblische Rede von Gott und die neuere Geschichtstheologie*. Wuppertal: Brockhaus, 1970.

Forbes, D. *The Liberal Anglican Idea of History*. Cambridge: Cambridge University Press, 1967.

France, Richard T. *Jesus and the Old Testament: His Application of Old Testament Passages to Himself and His Mission*. London: Tyndale, 1971.

France, Richard T., Wenham, David, and Blomberg, Craig, eds. *Gospel Perspectives*. 6 vols. Sheffield: JSOT, 1980–86.

Fuchs, Ernst. *Hermeneutik*. 4th ed. Tübingen: J. C. B. Mohr (Paul Siebeck), 1970.

―――. *Studies of the Historical Jesus*. Studies in Biblical Theology, no. 42. Trans. Andrew Scobie. London: SCM, 1964.

―――. *Zum hermeneutischen Problem in der Theologie: Die existentiale Interpretation*. 2d ed. Tübingen: J. C. B. Mohr (Paul Siebeck), 1965.

―――. *Zur Frage nach dem historischen Jesus*. Tübingen: J. C. B. Mohr (Paul Siebeck), 1960.

Fuller, Daniel. *Easter Faith and History*. Grand Rapids: Eerdmans, 1965; London: Inter-Varsity, 1968.

Funk, Robert W., ed. *History and Hermeneutic, Journal for Theology and the Church*. Vol. 4. New York: Harper & Row, 1967.

Gallagher, Eugene V. *Divine Man or Magician: Celsus and Origen on Jesus*. Society of Biblical Literature Dissertation Series 64. Chico, Calif.: Scholars, 1982.

Galloway, Alan D. *Wolfhart Pannenberg*. London: Allen & Unwin, 1973.

Geisler, Norman L. *Miracles and Modern Thought*. Grand Rapids: Zondervan, 1982.

Geisler, Norman L., ed. *Inerrancy*. Grand Rapids: Zondervan, 1979.

Gerdes, Hayo. *Das Christusbild Sören Kierkegaards*. Düsseldorf and Cologne: Diederichs, 1960.

———. *Sören Kierkegaard*. Berlin: Walter de Gruyter, 1966.

Gilkey, Langdon. *Reaping the Whirlwind: A Christian Interpretation of History*. New York: Seabury, 1976.

Goldingay, John. " 'That You May Know that Yahweh is God': A Study in the Relationship between Theology and Historical Truth in the Old Testament." *Tyndale Bulletin* 23 (1972): 58–93.

Gundry, Robert H. *The Use of the Old Testament in St. Matthew's Gospel with Special Reference to the Messianic Hope*. Supplements to *Novum Testamentum*, no. 18. Leiden: E. J. Brill, 1967.

Guttmann, Alexander, "The Significance of Miracles for Talmudic Judaism." *Hebrew Union College Annual* 20 (1947): 363–406. Reprinted in *Studies in Rabbinic Judaism*. New York: KTAV, 1976, pp. 47–90.

Hanson, Anthony Tyrrell. *The Living Utterances of God: The New Testament Exegesis of the Old*. London: Darton, Longman and Todd, 1983.

———. *Studies in Paul's Technique and Theology*. London: SPCK, 1974.

Hanson, Anthony Tyrrell, ed. *Vindications: Essays on the Historical Basis of Christianity*. London: SCM, 1966.

Hanson, Richard P. C. *Studies in Christian Antiquity*. Edinburgh: T. & T. Clark, 1985.

Harvey, A. E. *Jesus and the Constraints of History*. Bampton Lectures 1980. Philadelphia: Westminster; London: SPCK, 1982.

Harvey, Van Austin. *The Historian and the Believer: The Morality of Historical Knowledge and Christian Belief*. New York: Macmillan, 1966; London: SCM, 1967.

Helm, Paul. *The Varieties of Belief*. London: Allen & Unwin; New York: Humanities, 1973.

Hengel, Martin. *Acts and the History of Earliest Christianity*. Trans. John Bowden. London: SCM, 1979; Philadelphia: Fortress, 1980.

———. *Crucifixion: In the Ancient World and the Folly of the Message of the Cross*. Trans. John Bowden. Philadelphia: Fortress; London: SCM, 1977.

Henry, Carl F. H., ed. *Jesus of Nazareth: Saviour and Lord*. Grand Rapids: Eerdmans, 1966; London: Tyndale, 1967.

———. *Revelation and the Bible: Contemporary Evangelical Thought*. Grand Rapids: Eerdmans, 1958; London: Tyndale, 1959.

Hick, John. *Faith and the Philosophers*. New York: St. Martin's, 1964.

Hick, John, ed. *Faith and Knowledge*. 2d ed. Ithaca, N.Y.: Cornell University Press; London: Macmillan, 1967.

Hodges, H. A. *The Philosophy of Wilhem Dilthey*. London: Routledge & Kegan Paul, 1952.

Hoffmann, R. Joseph, and Larue, Gerald A., eds. *Jesus in History and Myth*. Buffalo: Prometheus Books, 1986.

Holland, R. F. "The Miraculous." *American Philosophical Quarterly* 2 (1965): 43–51. Reprinted in D. Z. Phillips, ed. *Religion and Understanding*. Oxford: Basil Blackwell, 1967, pp. 155–70.

Hollenbach, Paul W. "Jesus, Demoniacs, and Public Authorities: A Socio-Historical Study." *Journal of the American Academy of Religion* 49 (1981): 567–88.

Holladay, Carl H. *Theios Aner in Hellenistic Judaism. A Critique of the Use of this Category in New Testament Christology*. Society of Biblical Literature Dissertation Series 40. Missoula, Mont.: Scholars, 1977.

Hordern, William. *Introduction to Theology*. London: Lutterworth, 1968.

Hull, John M. *Hellenistic Magic and the Synoptic Tradition*. Studies in Biblical Theology. 2d ser., no. 28. London: SCM, 1974.

Hünermann, Peter. *Der Durchbruch geschichtlichen Denkens im 19. Jahrhundert*. Freiburg, Basel, and Vienna: Herder, 1967.

Jeremias, Joachim. *New Testament Theology*. Vol. 1. *The Proclamation of Jesus*. Trans. John Bowden. London: SCM; New York: Scribner, 1971.

———. *The Parables of Jesus*. Rev. ed. Trans. S. H. Hooke. London: SCM; New York: Scribner, 1963.

Johnson, Roger A. *The Origins of Demythologizing: Philosophy and Historiography in the Theology of Rudolf Bultmann*. Studies in the History of Religions (Supplements to *Numen*), no. 28. Leiden: E. J. Brill, 1974.

Kee, Howard Clark. *Miracle in the Early Christian World: A Study in Sociohistorical Method*. New Haven: Yale University Press, 1983.

Kegley, Charles W., ed. *The Theology of Rudolf Bultmann*. New York: Harper & Row; London: SCM, 1966.

Keller, Ernst, and Marie-Luise. *Miracles in Dispute: A Continuing Debate*. Trans. Margaret Kohl. London: SCM, 1969.

Kelsey, David H. *The Uses of Scripture in Recent Theology*. Philadelphia: Fortress, 1975.

Kierkegaard, Søren. *Concluding Unscientific Postscript to the Philosophical Fragments*. Trans. D. F. Swenson and Walter Lowrie. Princeton, N.J.: Princeton University Press, 1941.

———. *Philosophical Fragments; Johannes Climacus. Kierkegaard's Writings*. Vol. 7. Trans. Howard V. Hong and Edna H. Hong. Princeton: Princeton University Press, 1985.

———. *Training in Christianity*. Trans. Walter Lowrie. Princeton, N.J.: Princeton University Press, 1944.

Knox, John. *Criticism and Faith*. Nashville: Abingdon-Cokesbury, 1952; London: Hodder & Stoughton, 1953.

Kümmel, Werner Georg. *The New Testament: The History of the Investigation of its Problems*. Trans. S. McLean Gilmour and Howard C. Kee. Nashville: Abingdon, 1972.

Künneth, Walter. *The Theology of the Resurrection*. Trans. James W. Leitch. London: SCM, 1965.

Ladd, George Eldon. *I Believe in the Resurrection of Jesus*. Grand Rapids: Eerdmans; London: Hodder & Stoughton, 1975.

———. *The New Testament and Criticism*. Grand Rapids: Eerdmans, 1967; London: Hodder & Stoughton, 1970.

Lapide, Pinchas. *The Resurrection of Jesus: A Jewish Perspective.* Trans. Wilhelm C. Linss. Minneapolis: Augsburg, 1983.

Lawton, John Stewart. *Miracles and Revelation.* London: Lutterworth, 1959.

Lessing, Gotthold Ephraim. *Theological Writings.* Ed. Henry Chadwick. London: A. & C. Black; Stanford, Calif.: Stanford University Press, 1956.

Lewis, Clive Staples. *Miracles: A Preliminary Study.* London: Geoffrey Bles, 1947. Rev. paperback. London: Fontana Books, 1960.

Lewis, H. D. *Freedom and History.* London: Allen & Unwin, 1962.

Lindars, Barnabas. *New Testament Apologetic: The Doctrinal Significance of the Old Testament Quotations.* London: SCM, 1961.

Locke, John. *The Reasonableness of Christianity with a Discourse of Miracles.* Ed. Ian T. Ramsey. London: A. & C. Black; Stanford, Calif.: Stanford University Press, 1958.

Lonergan, Bernard J. F. *Method in Theology.* London: Darton, Longman & Todd, 1972.

Longenecker, Richard N. *Biblical Exegesis in the Apostolic Period.* Grand Rapids: Eerdmans, 1975.

_____. "Can We Reproduce the Exegesis of the New Testament?" *Tyndale Bulletin* 21 (1970): 3–38.

_____, and Tenney, Merrill C., eds., *New Dimensions in New Testament Study.* Grand Rapids: Zondervan, 1974.

Loos, H. van der. *The Miracles of Jesus.* Supplements to *Novum Testamentum,* no. 9. Leiden: E. J. Brill, 1965.

McArthur, Harvey K., ed. *In Search of the Historical Jesus.* New York: Scribner; London: SPCK, 1969.

McCarthy, Vincent A. *Quest for a Philosophical Jesus: Christianity and Philosophy in Rousseau, Kant, Hegel, and Schelling.* Macon, Ga.: Mercer University Press, 1986.

McIntire, C. T., ed. *God, History, and Historians.* New York: Oxford University Press, 1977.

McIntire, C. T., and Wells, Ronald, eds. *History and Historical Understanding.* Grand Rapids: Eerdmans, 1984.

McIntyre, John. *The Christian Doctrine of History.* Edinburgh: Oliver & Boyd, 1957.

_____. *The Shape of Christology.* London: SCM, 1966.

McKim, Donald K. *A Guide to Contemporary Hermeneutics: Major Trends in Biblical Interpretation.* Grand Rapids: Eerdmans, 1986.

_____. *What Christians Believe about the Bible.* Nashville: Thomas Nelson, 1985.

McKinnon, A. " 'Miracle' and 'Paradox.' " *American Philosophical Quarterly* 4 (1967): 301–14.

Macquarrie, John. *An Existentialist Theology: A Comparison of Heidegger and Bultmann.* London: SCM, 1955.

_____. *Principles of Christian Theology.* Rev. ed. New York: Scribner; London: SCM, 1977.

_____. *Twentieth-Century Religious Thought: The Frontiers of Philosophy and Theology, 1900–1980.* London: SCM; New York: Scribner, 1981.

Malet, André. *The Thought of Rudolf Bultmann*. Trans. Richard Strachan. Shannon: Irish University Press, 1969.

Marrou, Henri Irénée. *The Meaning of History*. Trans. Robert J. Olsen. Baltimore and Dublin: Helicon, 1966.

Marsden, George E., and Roberts, Frank, eds., *A Christian View of History*. Grand Rapids: Eerdmans, 1975.

Marshall, I. Howard, ed. *New Testament Interpretation: Essays on Principles and Methods*. Grand Rapids: Eerdmans; Exeter: Paternoster, 1977.

Marxsen, Willi. *The Resurrection of Jesus of Nazareth*. Trans. Margaret Kohl. London: SCM, 1970.

Mascall, E. L. *Christian Theology and Natural Science: Some Questions in Their Relations*. Bampton Lectures, 1956. London: Longmans, Green and Co. 1956.

―――. *The Christian Universe*. London: Darton, Longman & Todd, 1966.

―――. *The Openness of Being: Natural Theology Today*. London: Darton, Longman & Todd, 1971.

―――. *Theology and the Future*. London: Darton, Longman & Todd, 1968.

Meinhold, Peter. *Geschichte der kirchlichen Historiographie*, 2 vols. Munich: Karl Alber Verlag, 1967.

Meynell, Hugo A. *An Introduction to the Philosophy of Bernard Lonergan*. London and New York: Macmillan, 1976.

―――. *The Theology of Bernard Lonergan*. American Academy of Religion Studies in Religion, no. 42. Atlanta: Scholars, 1986.

Michalson, Carl. *The Hinge of History: An Existential Approach to the Christian Faith*. New York: Scribner, 1959.

Michalson, Gordon E., Jr. *The Historical Dimensions of a Rational Faith: The Role of History in Kant's Religious Thought*. Washington, D.C: University Press of America, 1977.

―――. *Lessing's "Ugly Ditch": A Study of Theology and History*. University Park and London: The Pennsylvania State University Press, 1985.

―――. "Pannenberg on the Resurrection and Historical Method." *Scottish Journal of Theology* 33 (1980): 345–61.

Middleton, Conyers. *A Free Inquiry into the Miraculous Powers which are Supposed to have Subsisted in the Christian Church, from the Earliest Ages through Several Successive Centuries*. 1784. London: Sherwood and Co., 1825.

Moltmann, Jürgen. *Hope and Planning*. Trans. Margaret Clarkson. New York: Harper & Row; London: SCM, 1971.

―――. *Theology of Hope: On the Ground and Implications of a Christian Eschatology*. Trans. James W. Leitch. New York: Harper & Row; London: SCM, 1967.

Montgomery, John Warwick. *History in Christian Perspective*. Vol. 1. *The Shape of the Past: An Introduction to Philosophical Historiography*. Ann Arbor: Edwards Brothers, 1962.

Morris, Leon. *The Gospel According to John*. Grand Rapids: Eerdmans, 1971.

Moule, C. F. D. *The Phenomenon of the New Testament: An Inquiry into the Implications of Certain Features of the New Testament*. Studies in Biblical Theology. 2d ser., no. 1. London: A. & C. Black, 1967.

Moule, C. F. D., ed. *Miracles: Cambridge Studies in Their Philosophy and History*. London: Mowbray, 1965.

_____. *The Significance of the Message of the Resurrection for Faith in Jesus Christ.* Studies in Biblical Theology. 2d ser., no. 8. London: SCM, 1968.

Moule, C. F. D., and Cuppit, D. "The Resurrection: A Disagreement." *Theology* 75 (1972): 507–19.

Nash, Ronald H. *Christian Faith and Historical Understanding.* Grand Rapids: Zondervan, 1984.

Navone, John J. *History and Faith in the Thought of Alan Richardson.* London: SCM, 1966.

Neill, Stephen. *The Interpretation of the New Testament, 1861–1961.* Firth Lectures, 1962. London: Oxford University Press, 1964.

Niebuhr, Reinhold. *Beyond Tragedy: Essays on the Christian Interpretation of History.* New York: Scribner, 1937.

_____. *Faith and History: A Comparison of Christian and Modern Views of History.* New York: Scribner, 1949.

_____. *The Irony of American History.* New York: Scribner, 1952.

_____. *The Nature and Destiny of Man: A Christian Interpretation.* Gifford Lectures, 1939. 2 vols. New York: Scribner; London: Nisbet, 1941–43.

_____. *The Self and the Dramas of History.* New York: Scribner, 1955.

Niebuhr, Richard R. *Resurrection and Historical Reason: A Study of Theological Method.* New York: Scribner, 1957.

Nygren, Anders. *Meaning and Method: Prolegomena to a Scientific Philosophy of Religion and a Scientific Theology.* Trans. Philip S. Watson. London: Epworth, 1972.

Olive, Don H. *Wolfhart Pannenberg.* Makers of the Modern Theological Mind. Waco, Tex.: Word Books, 1973.

Orr, James. *The Resurrection of Jesus.* London: Hodder & Stoughton, 1908.

Owen, H. P. *The Christian Knowledge of God.* London: University of London Press, Athlone, 1969.

_____. *Concepts of Deity.* London and New York: Macmillan, 1971.

_____. *Revelation and Existence: A Study in the Theology of Rudolf Bultmann.* Cardiff: University of Wales Press, 1957.

Palmer, Humphrey. *The Logic of Gospel Criticism: An Account of the Methods and Arguments Used by Textual, Documentary, Source, and Form Critics of the New Testament.* London and New York: Macmillan, 1968.

Pannenberg, Wolfhart. *The Apostles' Creed in the Light of Today's Questions.* Trans. Margaret Kohl. Philadelphia: Westminster; London: SCM, 1972.

_____. *Basic Questions in Theology.* 3 vols. Vols. 1 and 2 trans. George H. Kehm; vol. 3 trans. R. A. Wilson. London: SCM, 1970–73. U.S. ed. of vols. 1 and 2. Philadelphia: Fortress. U.S. ed. of vol. 3 published under the title *The Idea of God and Human Freedom.* Philadelphia: Westminster.

_____. *Jesus—God and Man.* Trans. Lewis L Wilkins and Duane E. Priebe. London: SCM; Philadelphia: Westminster, 1968. 2d ed. 1970.

Pannenberg, Wolfhart, ed. *Revelation as History.* Trans. David Granskou and Edward Quinn. New York: Macmillan, 1968; London: Sheed and Ward, 1969.

Pauck, Wilhelm. *Harnack and Troeltsch: Two Historical Theologians.* New York: Oxford University Press, 1968.

Ramsey, A. M. *The Resurrection of Christ: A Study of the Event and its Meaning for the Christian Faith.* Paperback. London: Fontana Books, 1961.

Ramsey, Ian T. *Christian Empiricism.* Ed. Jerry H. Gill. London: Sheldon, 1974.

————. *Religious Language: An Empirical Placing of Theological Phrases.* London: SCM, 1957.

Ramsey, Ian T., ed. *Christian Ethics and Contemporary Philosophy.* London: SCM, 1966.

————. *Words about God: The Philosophy of Religion.* London: SCM, 1971.

Ramsey, Ian T., et al. *The Miracles and the Resurrection: Some Recent Studies.* SPCK Theological Collections, no. 3. London: SPCK, 1964.

Reimarus, Hermann Samuel. *Reimarus: Fragments.* Ed. C. H. Talbert, trans. Ralph S. Fraser. Philadelphia: Fortress; London: SCM, 1971.

Reist, Benjamin A. *Toward a Theology of Involvement: A Study of Ernst Troeltsch.* Philadelphia: Westminster; London: SCM, 1966.

Reumann, John Henry Paul. *Jesus in the Church's Gospels: Modern Scholarship and the Earliest Sources.* Philadelphia: Fortress; London: SPCK, 1970.

Reventlow, Henning Graf. *The Authority of the Bible and the Rise of the Modern World.* Trans. John Bowden. Philadelphia: Fortress; London: SCM, 1985.

————. *Problems of Biblical Theology in the Twentieth Century.* Philadelphia: Fortress; London: SCM, 1986.

————. *Problems of Old Testament Theology in the Twentieth Century.* Trans. John Bowden. Philadelphia: Fortress; London: SCM, 1985.

Richardson, Alan. *The Bible in the Age of Science.* Cadbury Lectures, 1961. London: SCM, 1961.

————. *Christian Apologetics.* London: SCM, 1947; New York: Harper, 1948.

————. *History: Sacred and Profane.* Bampton Lectures, 1962. London: SCM, 1964.

————. *An Introduction to the Theology of the New Testament.* London: SCM; New York: Harper, 1958.

————. *The Miracle-Stories of the Gospels.* London: SCM, 1941.

Riesner, Rainer. *Jesus als Lehrer. Eine Untersuchung zum Ursprung der Evangelien.* Wissenschaftliche Untersuchungen zum Neuen Testament, 2. Reihe 7. Tübingen: J. C. B. Mohr (Paul Siebeck), 1981.

Ristow, Helmut, and Matthiae, Karl, eds. *Der historische Jesus und der kerygmatische Christus. Beiträge zum Christusverständnis im Forschung und Verkündigung.* 2d ed. Berlin: Evangelische Verlaganstalt, 1962.

Roberts, T. A. "The Historian and the Believer." *Religious Studies* 7 (1971): 251–57.

————. *History and Christian Apologetic.* London: SPCK, 1960.

Robinson, James M. *A New Quest of the Historical Jesus and Other Essays.* Philadelphia: Fortress, 1983.

————. *Theology as History,* New Frontiers in Theology, no. 3. New York: Harper & Row, 1967.

Robinson, James M., ed. *The Future of Our Religious Past: Essays in Honour of Rudolf Bultmann.* Trans. Charles E. Carlston and Robert P. Scharlemann. New York: Harper & Row; London: SCM, 1971.

Robinson, James M., and Cobb, J. B., eds. *The New Hermeneutic*. New Frontiers in Theology, no. 2. New York: Harper & Row, 1964.

Robinson, J. A. T. "Resurrection in the NT," in G. A. Buttrick et al., eds. *The Interpreter's Dictionary of the Bible*. 5 vols. New York and Nashville: Abingdon, 1962–76, 4:43–53.

Rogers, Jack B., and McKim, Donald K. *The Authority and Interpretation of the Bible: An Historical Approach*. San Francisco: Harper & Row, 1979.

Rudolf, Kurt. *Gnosis: The Nature of Christian Gnosticism*. Trans. R. M. Wilson. San Francisco: Harper & Row, 1983.

Ruegsegger, Ronald W., ed. *Reflections on Francis Schaeffer*. Grand Rapids: Zondervan, 1986.

Rust, Eric C. *Towards a Theological Understanding of History*. New York: Oxford University Press, 1963.

Sanders, E. P. *The Tendencies of the Synoptic Tradition*. Society for New Testament Studies Monograph Series, no. 9, Cambridge: Cambridge University Press, 1965.

_____. *Jesus and Judaism*. Philadelphia: Fortress, 1985.

Schaeffer, Francis. *Escape from Reason*. London and Downers Grove: InterVarsity Press, 1968.

_____. *The God Who Is There*. London: Hodder & Stoughton; Downers Grove: InterVarsity, 1968.

_____. *He Is There and He Is not Silent*. London: Hodder and Stoughton; Wheaton: Tyndale, 1972.

Schmithals, Walter. *An Introduction to the Theology of Rudolf Bultmann*. Trans. John Bowden. London: SCM; Minneapolis: Augsburg, 1968.

Schüssler-Fiorenza, Elizabeth, ed. *Aspects of Religious Propaganda in Judaism and Early Christianity*. University of Notre Dame Center for the Study of Judaism and Christianity in Antiquity, no. 2. Notre Dame: University of Notre Dame Press, 1976.

Schweitzer, Albert. *The Quest of the Historical Jesus: A Critical Study of its Progress from Reimarus to Wrede*. Trans. from 1st German ed. by W. Montgomery. 1910. Paperback. New York: Macmillan: 1968.

Seeberg, Reinhold. "Wunder." *Realenzyklopädie für Protestantische Theologie und Kirche*. Ed. A. Hauck. Leipzig: J. C. Hinrich'sche Buchhandlung, 1908. 21:558–67.

Shinn, Roger Lincoln. *Christianity and the Problem of History*. New York: Scribner, 1953.

Shorter, Aylward. *Jesus and the Witchdoctor: Approach to Healing and Wholeness*. London: Geoffrey Chapman; Maryknoll, N.Y.: Orbis Books, 1985.

Smith, Morton. *Jesus the Magician*. San Francisco: Harper & Row, 1978.

Soulen, Richard N. *Handbook of Biblical Criticism*. Rev. ed. Atlanta: John Knox, 1981.

Sponheim, Paul. *Kierkegaard on Christ and Christian Coherence*. New York: Harper & Row; London: SCM, 1968.

Stendahl, Krister. *The School of St. Matthew and its Use of the Old Testament*. Acta Seminarii Neotestamentici Upsaliensis 20. 2d ed. Lund: C. W. K. Gleerup, 1967.

Stauffer, Ethelbert. *Jerusalem und Rom im Zeitalter Jesu.* Bern: Francke Verlage, 1957.

———. *Jesus and His Story.* English trans. by Dorothea M. Barton. London: SCM, 1960. American trans. by Richard Winston and Clara Winston. New York: Alfred A. Knopf, 1960.

Strobel, August. *Die Stunde der Wahrheit. Untersuchungen zum Strafverfahren gegen Jesu.* Wissenschaftliche Untersuchungen zum Neuen Testament, 2 Reihe 21. Tübingen: J. C. B. Mohr (Paul Siebeck), 1980.

Swinburne, Richard. *The Coherence of Theism.* Oxford: Clarendon, 1977.

———. *The Concept of Miracle.* London and New York: Macmillan, St. Martin's, 1970.

———. *The Existence of God.* Oxford: Clarendon, 1979.

———. *Faith and Reason.* Oxford: Clarendon, 1981.

Sykes, S. W., and Clayton, J. P., eds., *Christ, Faith and History: Cambridge Studies in Christology.* Cambridge: Cambridge University Press, 1972.

Talbert, C. H. *What is a Gospel? The Genre of the Canonical Gospels.* Philadelphia: Fortress, 1977.

Thiselton, Anthony C. "Kierkegaard and the Nature of Truth." *The Churchman* 89 (1975): 85–105.

———. *The Two Horizons: New Testament Hermeneutics and Philosophical Description.* Grand Rapids: Eerdmans; Exeter: Paternoster, 1980.

Tiede, David Lenz. *The Charismatic Figure as Miracle Worker.* Society of Biblical Literature Dissertation Series 1. Missoula, Mont.: Society of Biblical Literature, 1972.

Tillich, Paul. *The Interpretation of History.* New York: Scribner, 1936.

———. *Systematic Theology,* 3 vols. Chicago: University of Chicago Press, 1951–63. English ed. London: Nisbet, 1953–64.

Torrance, Thomas Forsyth. *God and Rationality.* London and New York: Oxford University Press, 1971.

———. *Space, Time and Incarnation.* London and New York: Oxford University Press, 1969.

———. *Theological Science.* London and New York: Oxford University Press, 1969.

———. *Theology in Reconstruction.* London: SCM, 1965; Grand Rapids: Eerdmans, 1966.

———. *Transformation and Convergence in the Frame of Knowledge: Explorations in the Interrelations of Scientific and Theological Enterprise.* Belfast: Christian Journal; Grand Rapids: Eerdmans, 1984.

Troeltsch, Ernst. *The Absoluteness of Christianity and the History of Religions.* Trans. David Reid. Richmond: John Knox, 1971; London: SCM, 1972.

———. *Christian Thought: Its History and Application.* Ed. Baron F. von Hügel, 1923; New York: Meridian Books, 1957.

———. *Ernst Troeltsch: Writings on Theology and Religion.* Trans. and ed. Robert Morgan and Michael Pye. Atlanta: John Knox, 1977.

———. *Gesammelte Schriften,* 4 vols. (1912–25). Tübingen: J. C. B. Mohr (Paul Siebeck). Reprint of 2d ed. Aalen: Scientia Verlag, 1981.

_____. "Historiography." *Encyclopaedia of Religion and Ethics.* Ed. James Hastings. Edinburgh: T. & T. Clark, 1914: 4:716–23.

Trotter, F. Thomas, ed. *Jesus and the Historian. Written in Honor of Ernest Cadman Colwell.* Philadelphia: Westminster, 1968.

Tupper, E. Frank. *The Theology of Wolfhart Pannenberg.* Postscript by Wolfhart Pannenberg. Philadelphia: Westminster, 1973; London: SCM, 1974.

Tuttle, Howard Nelson. *Wilhelm Dilthey's Philosophy of Historical Understanding: A Critical Analysis.* Leiden: E. J. Brill, 1969.

Tyrell, Bernard. *Bernard Lonergan's Philosophy of God.* Dublin: Gill and Macmillan, 1974.

Vermes, Geza. *Jesus the Jew: A Historian's Reading of the Gospels.* London: Collins, 1969. 2d ed., 1983.

_____. *Jesus and the World of Judaism.* Philadelphia: Fortress, 1984.

_____. *Post-Biblical Jewish Studies.* Studies in Judaism in Late Antiquity, no. 8. Leiden: E. J. Brill, 1975.

Warfield, B. B. *The Inspiration and Authority of the Bible.* Philadelphia: Presbyterian and Reformed Publishing Company, 1948; London: Marshall, Morgan & Scott, 1951.

_____. *Miracles: Yesterday and Today, True and False.* Grand Rapids: Eerdmans, 1954. First published under the title *Counterfeit Miracles.* New York: Scribner, 1918.

Weeden, Theodore J., Sr. *Mark: Traditions in Conflict.* Philadelphia: Fortress, 1971. Reprint 1979.

Wells, G. A. *Did Jesus Exist?* London: Elek/Pemberton, 1975.

_____. *The Jesus of the Early Christians: A Study of Christian Origins.* London: Pemberton Books, 1961.

Wenham, J. W. *Christ and the Bible,* Leicester: Inter-Varsity, 1972.

Wilson, Ian. *Jesus: The Evidence.* San Francisco: Harper & Row, 1984.

Wilson, R. M. *Gnosis and the New Testament.* Philadelphia: Fortress, 1968.

Woodbridge, John D. *Biblical Authority: A Critique of the Rogers/McKim Proposal.* Grand Rapids: Zondervan, 1982.

Wright, G. Ernest. *God who Acts: Biblical Theology as Recital.* Studies in Biblical Theology, no. 8. London: SCM, 1952.

Wright, J. Stafford, and Brown, Colin. "Magic, Sorcery, Magi." *The New International Dictionary of New Testament Theology.* Ed. Colin Brown. 2:552–62.

Yamauchi, Edwin M. "Magic or Miracle? Diseases, Demons and Exorcisms," in *Gospel Perspectives,* vol. 6. *The Miracles of Jesus,* pp. 89–183.

_____. *Pre-Christian Gnosticism: A Survey of the Proposed Evidence.* 2d ed. Grand Rapids: Baker, 1983.

Young, W. *History and Existential Theology: The Role of History in the Thought of Rudolf Bultmann.* Philadelphia: Westminster, 1969.

Youngblood, Ronald, ed. *Evangelicals and Inerrancy.* Nashville: Thomas Nelson, 1984.

Zahrnt, Heinz. *The Historical Jesus.* Trans. John Bowden. London: Collins; New York: Harper & Row, 1963.

_____. *The Question of God: Protestant Theology in the Twentieth Century.* Trans. R. A. Wilson. London: Collins, 1969.

Index of Authors

For further details see also the Select Bibliography.

Index of Subjects